Dessert First!

Life's Uncertain... Eat Dessert First!

Distributed By:

Products

507 Industrial Street
Waverly, IA 50677

ISBN 1-56383-190-2
Item #7055

Table of Contents

Cookies

Two-Chip Chocolate Chip Cookies

Makes 5 dozen

1 C. shortening
3/4 C. sugar
3/4 C. brown sugar
1 tsp. vanilla
2 eggs

2 1/4 C. flour
1 tsp. baking soda
1/4 tsp. salt
1 C. chocolate chips
1 C. white chocolate chips

Preheat oven to 350°. In a medium bowl, cream together shortening, sugar and brown sugar. Add vanilla and eggs and mix well. Into a separate bowl, sift flour, baking soda and salt. Add sifted ingredients to creamed mixture. Mix in chocolate chips and white chocolate chips. Drop dough by tablespoonfuls onto greased baking sheets. Bake in oven for 7 to 10 minutes or until cookies are golden brown. Let cookies cool on baking sheet for 5 minutes before removing to a wire rack. Store in an airtight container.

Big Soft Ginger Cookies

Makes 2 dozen

2 1/4 C. flour
2 tsp. ground ginger
1 tsp. baking soda
3/4 tsp. cinnamon
1/2 tsp. ground cloves
1/4 tsp. salt

3/4 C. margarine, softened
1 C. plus 2 T. sugar, divided
1 egg
1 T. water
1/4 C. molasses

Preheat oven to 350°. Into a large bowl, sift flour, ground ginger, baking soda, cinnamon, ground cloves and salt. In a separate large bowl, cream together margarine and 1 cup sugar, mixing until lightened and fluffy. Beat in egg and stir in water and molasses. Gradually stir in sifted ingredients and mix well. Shape tablespoonfuls of dough into rounded balls. Place remaining 2 tablespoons sugar in a shallow bowl. Roll balls in sugar and place, 2" apart, onto ungreased baking sheets. Bake in oven for 8 to 10 minutes. Let cookies cool on baking sheet for 5 minutes before removing to a wire rack. Store in an airtight container.

Delicious Peanut Butter Cookies

Makes 4 dozen

1/2 C. shortening	1 T. vanilla
1 1/4 C. brown sugar	1 3/4 C. flour
3/4 C. peanut butter	3/4 tsp. baking soda
1 egg	3/4 tsp. salt
3 T. milk	

Preheat oven to 375°. In a medium bowl, cream together shortening, brown sugar and peanut butter until smooth. Stir in egg, milk and vanilla. In a separate bowl, combine flour, baking soda and salt. Stir dry ingredients into creamed mixture, mixing until well blended. Drop dough by tablespoonfuls onto ungreased baking sheets. Bake in oven for 8 to 10 minutes. Let cookies cool on baking sheet for 5 minutes before removing to a wire rack. Store in an airtight container.

Apricot and White Chocolate Chip Cookies

Makes 3 dozen

1 2/3 C. flour
1/2 tsp. baking soda
1/4 tsp. salt
3/4 C. butter, softened
1 C. brown sugar

1 tsp. vanilla
1 egg
2 C. white chocolate chips
3/4 C. chopped almonds
3/4 C. chopped dried apricots

Preheat oven to 350°. In a medium bowl, sift together flour, baking soda and salt. In a large bowl, cream together butter and brown sugar until smooth. Beat in vanilla and egg. Add dry ingredients and mix until well blended. Stir in white chocolate chips, chopped almonds and dried apricots. Mix well and drop dough by teaspoonfuls onto ungreased baking sheets. Bake in oven for 10 to 12 minutes, until cookies are golden brown. Remove from oven and transfer cookies to wire racks to cool.

Orange Poppyseed Cookies

Makes 5 dozen

1/3 C. butter	1/4 C. cornstarch
3/4 C. sugar	1/4 tsp. baking soda
1 egg	1 T. buttermilk
1 1/2 tsp. grated orange peel	2 T. poppy seeds
2 tsp. orange juice	1 C. white chocolate chips
1 C. flour	

Preheat oven to 350°. In a medium bowl, cream together butter, sugar and egg until lightened and fluffy. Stir in grated orange peel and orange juice. Into a separate bowl, sift flour, cornstarch and baking soda. Add sifted ingredients to creamed mixture. Mix in buttermilk and poppy seeds, stirring to form a soft dough. Drop dough by tablespoonfuls onto greased baking sheets. Press a single white chocolate chip into the center of each cookie. Bake in oven for 15 minutes or until cookies are golden brown. Let cookies cool on baking sheet for 5 minutes before removing to a wire rack. Store in an airtight container.

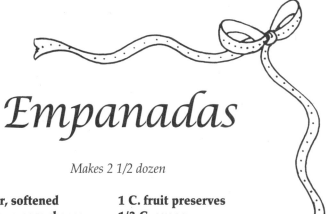

Empanadas

Makes 2 1/2 dozen

1/2 C. butter, softened	**1 C. fruit preserves**
1 (3 oz.) pkg. cream cheese,	**1/3 C. sugar**
softened	**1 tsp. cinnamon**
1 C. flour, sifted	

In a medium bowl, cream together butter and cream cheese until smooth and well blended. Add flour and beat until smooth. Shape dough into a round ball and wrap in aluminum foil or plastic wrap and refrigerate overnight. Remove dough from refrigerator 30 minutes prior to using. Preheat oven to 375°. On a flat, lightly floured surface, roll chilled dough very thin. Using a 3" or 4" round cookie cutter, cut dough into rounds. Place a small spoonful of fruit preserves in the center of each round and moisten the edges with water. Fold round over in half and press the edges together. Place empanadas on an ungreased baking sheet and bake in oven for 15 to 20 minutes. Place sugar and cinnamon in a shallow dish and mix together. Remove cookies from oven and immediately roll in sugar/cinnamon mixture.

Hawaiian Tarts

Makes 3 dozen

1 C. butter, softened	2 T. cornstarch
1 tsp. vanilla	1 C. pineapple preserves
1/2 C. plus 1/3 C. powdered	1/2 C. sugar
sugar, divided	1 egg
1 3/4 C. flour	1 1/2 C. shredded coconut

Preheat oven to 350°. In a large bowl, cream together butter, vanilla and 1/2 cup powdered sugar, mixing until smooth. Into a separate bowl, sift flour and cornstarch. Add sifted mixture to creamed mixture and stir until a dough forms. Roll dough into 1" balls and press 1 ball into each cup of greased miniature muffin tins. Press dough onto bottom and up sides of muffin tins to form cups. Place 1 teaspoon pineapple preserves in each cup. In a small bowl, combine sugar and egg, mixing until well blended. Stir in shredded coconut. Place 1 teaspoon coconut mixture over pineapple in each cup. Bake in oven for 25 to 30 minutes, until slightly golden brown. Let tarts cool in pan for 15 minutes. Lightly tap the muffin tins on the counter to loosen tarts. Before serving, dust tarts with remaining 1/3 cup powdered sugar.

Dixie Sugar Cookies

Makes 3 to 4 dozen

1/2 C. shortening	2 eggs, beaten
1/4 tsp. salt	2 T. milk
1/2 tsp. grated lemon peel	2 C. flour
1/2 tsp. nutmeg	1 tsp. baking powder
1 C. sugar	1/2 T. baking soda

Preheat oven to 375°. Line baking sheets with parchment paper and set aside. In a large bowl, combine shortening, salt, grated lemon peel and nutmeg. Add sugar and beat well. Add eggs and milk and mix until well combined. Into a separate bowl, sift flour, baking powder and baking soda. Add sifted ingredients to creamed mixture and mix well. Drop dough by teaspoonfuls onto prepared baking sheets. Flatten each cookie with the bottom of a glass and sprinkle tops of cookies with additional sugar. Bake in oven for 8 to 12 minutes. Let cookies cool on baking sheet for 5 minutes before removing to a wire rack.

Nutty Mocha Cookies

Makes 3 dozen

1/2 C. butter, softened	1 1/2 tsp. baking powder
1/2 C. cocoa powder	1/4 tsp. salt
3 large eggs, room temperature	6 oz. white chocolate, coarsely
3/4 C. sugar	chopped
1/2 C. brown sugar	6 oz. chocolate chips
1 T. vanilla	1 C. coarsely chopped pecans,
2 T. coffee-flavored liqueur	toasted*
2 1/2 C. flour	

Line baking sheets with parchment paper and set aside. In a large glass bowl, place butter. Microwave on high for 30 seconds at a time, until melted. Using a wire whisk, mix in cocoa powder, whisking until smooth. In a medium mixing bowl, beat together eggs, sugar and brown sugar at medium speed for 4 to 5 minutes. Scrape sides of bowl, add melted butter mixture and beat until smooth. Add vanilla and coffee-flavored liqueur and beat until smooth. In a separate bowl, combine flour, baking powder and salt. Add flour mixture to butter mixture and beat at low speed just until combined. Stir in chopped white chocolate, chocolate chips and pecans, mixing until combined. Chill dough in refrigerator for at least 1 hour, until firm. Preheat oven to 325°. Divide dough into 4 equal pieces and shape each piece into a 1 1/2" by 8" log. Place logs, 2" apart, on prepared baking sheets. Bake in oven for 25 to 30 minutes, until tops are cracked and a toothpick inserted in center of logs comes out clean. Transfer logs to a cutting board and let cool for 15 minutes. Cut each log into 1" slices. Store cookies in an airtight container.

* To toast, place chopped pecans in a single layer on a baking sheet. Bake at 350° for approximately 10 minutes or until pecans are golden brown.

Oatmeal Raisin Cookies

Makes 3 1/2 dozen

2 1/4 C. flour
1/2 C. quick oats
3/4 tsp. baking soda
1/2 tsp. salt
1 1/2 C. dark brown sugar

1 C. butter, softened,
    cut into pieces
2 large eggs, room temperature
1 T. vanilla
1 1/2 C. raisins

In a large bowl, combine flour, oats, baking soda and salt. In a medium mixing bowl, beat brown sugar and medium speed until fluffy. Add pieces of butter, several at a time, and beat until combined. In a small bowl, lightly mix eggs and vanilla. Add eggs mixture to butter mixture and beat at low speed until smooth. Add flour mixture and beat until just combined. Mix in raisins until evenly incorporated. Chill dough in refrigerator for at least 1 hour, until firm. Preheat oven to 300°. Drop dough by teaspoonfuls onto ungreased baking sheets. Bake in oven for 22 to 23 minutes or until cookies are slightly soft and edges are light golden in color. Remove cookies to a wire rack to cool. Store in an airtight container.

Almond and Chocolate Nugget Cookies

Makes about 3 dozen

1 1/3 C. plus 3 T. flour
1/8 tsp. baking soda
1/8 tsp. cream of tartar
1/4 tsp. salt
1/2 C. butter, softened
2 T. plus 2 tsp. shortening
2/3 C. brown sugar
1/3 C. sugar

1 large egg
1 tsp. almond extract
3/4 tsp. vanilla
12 oz. bittersweet chocolate, chopped
1 C. shredded coconut
2/3 C. slivered almonds, toasted*

Preheat oven to 325°. Line baking sheets with parchment paper and set aside. In a small mixing bowl, combine flour, baking soda, cream of tartar and salt. In a large mixing bowl, cream butter and shortening at low speed for 2 minutes. Add brown sugar and beat for 1 additional minute. Add sugar and mix well. Blend in egg, almond extract and vanilla. Add flour mixture to creamed mixture, beating at low speed. Fold in chopped chocolate, shredded coconut and toasted almonds. Drop dough by 2-tablespoonfuls, 3" apart, onto prepared baking sheets. Bake in oven for 16 to 18 minutes or until cookies are pale golden in color. Remove cookies to a wire rack to cool. Store in an airtight container.

* To toast, place slivered almonds in a single layer on a baking sheet. Bake at 350° for approximately 7 minutes or until almonds are lightly toasted.

Cashew Butter Cookies

Makes 4 1/2 dozen

3/4 C. butter, softened
1/2 C. brown sugar
1/2 C. honey
1 egg
2 C. flour

3/4 tsp. baking soda
1/2 tsp. baking powder
1 C. chopped salted cashews
Cashew halves

Preheat oven to 375°. In a large mixing bowl, combine butter, brown sugar, honey and egg. Beat at medium speed for 1 to 2 minutes, until well mixed. Reduce speed to low and add flour, baking soda and baking powder. Continue beating for 1 to 2 minutes and stir in chopped cashews by hand. Drop dough by teaspoonfuls onto a greased baking sheet. Top each cookie with a cashew half. Bake in oven for 6 to 9 minutes or until cookies are golden brown.

Macadamia Nut White Chocolate Chunk Cookies

Makes 2 dozen

3/4 C. brown sugar
1/2 C. butter, softened
1 egg
1 1/2 tsp. vanilla
1 1/3 C. flour
1/2 tsp. baking powder
1/2 tsp. baking soda

1/2 tsp. salt
2 (3 oz.) bar white chocolate, cut into 1/2" pieces
1 (3 1/2 oz. jar salted macadamia nuts, coarsely chopped

Preheat oven to 350°. In a large mixing bowl, combine brown sugar, butter, egg and vanilla. Beat at medium speed for 1 to 2 minutes, until well mixed. Reduce speed to low and add flour, baking powder, baking soda and salt. Continue beating for an additional 1 to 2 minutes, until well mixed. Stir in white chocolate pieces and chopped macadamia nuts by hand. Drop dough by tablespoonfuls, 2" apart, onto greased baking sheets. Bake in oven for 9 to 12 minutes or until cookies are light golden brown. Let cool on baking sheets for 1 minute before removing to wire racks.

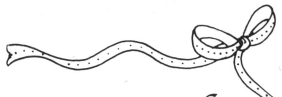

Butterscotch Oatmeal Cookies

Makes 3 1/2 dozen

2 C. flour
2 tsp. baking powder
3/4 tsp. baking soda
1 tsp. salt
3/4 tsp. nutmeg
1/8 tsp. ground allspice
1 C. butter, softened
1 C. brown sugar

1/2 C. sugar
2 large eggs
2 1/2 tsp. vanilla
1 T. hot water
1 1/2 C. quick cooking oats
2 C. butterscotch chips
3/4 C. chopped walnuts

Preheat oven to 375°. Grease or line baking sheets with parchment paper and set aside. Into a large bowl, sift flour, baking powder, baking soda, salt, nutmeg and allspice. In a large mixing bowl, cream butter at low speed for 4 minutes. Add brown sugar and beat at medium speed for 1 minute. Add sugar and beat for an additional minute. Blend in eggs, one at a time, beating for 1 minute after each addition. Add vanilla and hot water and mix well. Reduce speed to low and add sifted flour mixture. Add oats and blend until well mixed. The dough should be thick and moderately stiff. Mix in butterscotch chips and chopped walnuts by hand. Drop dough by tablespoonfuls, 3" apart, onto prepared baking sheets. Bake in oven for 10 to 12 minutes or until light golden brown.

Cinnamon Coffee Cookies

Makes 8 dozen

1 C. brown sugar
3/4 C. butter, softened
1/4 C. plus 3 T. orange juice, divided
1 T. grated orange peel
2 3/4 C. flour
1 T. plus 3/4 tsp. instant espresso powder, divided

1 3/4 tsp. baking powder
1 tsp. cinnamon
1/2 tsp. salt
1/2 C. finely chopped pecans
1 1/2 C. powdered sugar
96 chocolate-covered coffee beans, optional

In a large mixing bowl, combine brown sugar and butter. Beat at medium speed for 1 to 2 minutes, until creamy. Add 1/4 cup orange juice and grated orange peel and beat for 1 to 2 minutes, until well mixed. Reduce speed to low and add flour, 1 tablespoon instant espresso powder, baking powder, cinnamon, salt and finely chopped pecans. Divide dough in half and shape each half into a 15" log, about 1 1/4" in diameter. Cover logs in plastic wrap and chill in refrigerator for 1 hour. Preheat oven to 375°. Remove logs from refrigerator and cut each log into 1/4" slices and place 1" apart on lightly greased baking sheets. Flatten each cookie slightly with the bottom of a glass. Bake in oven for 6 to 8 minutes. Meanwhile, in a small bowl, combine powdered sugar and remaining 3/4 teaspoon instant espresso powder. Gradually mix in remaining 3 tablespoons orange juice. Remove cookies from oven and let cool slightly. Spoon about 1/4 teaspoon glaze over each warm cookie. Lightly press 1 chocolate-covered coffee bean on top of each cookie, if desired.

Banana Chocolate Chip Bars

Makes 2 dozen

3/4 C. butter, softened	1 C. mashed bananas
2/3 C. sugar	1 3/4 C. flour
2/3 C. brown sugar	2 tsp. baking powder
1 egg, beaten	1/2 tsp. salt
1 tsp. vanilla	1 C. chocolate chips

Preheat oven to 350°. Grease and flour a 10x15" jelly roll pan. In a large bowl, cream together butter, sugar and brown sugar until fluffy. Beat in egg and vanilla and fold in mashed bananas. In a separate bowl, combine flour, baking powder and salt. Fold flour mixture into butter mixture. Stir in chocolate chips. Spread mixture into prepared pan. Bake in oven for 20 minutes, until set. Remove from oven and let cool before cutting into bars.

Apricot-Coconut Squares

Makes 2 dozen

1/2 C. butter, softened	1/4 tsp. salt
1/4 C. sugar	1 tsp. vanilla
1 1/3 C. flour, divided	1 tsp. lemon juice
2/3 C. dried apricots	1 C. chopped walnuts
1 C. water	3/4 C. shredded coconut,
2 eggs	optional
1 C. brown sugar	1/3 C. powdered sugar
1/2 tsp. baking powder	

Preheat oven to 325°. In a medium bowl, combine butter, sugar and 1 cup flour. Mix well and press mixture into the bottom of an ungreased 9x13" baking dish. Bake in oven for 25 minutes. In a small saucepan, combine dried apricots and water. Bring to a boil and cook for 10 minutes. Drain saucepan, chopped apricots and set aside. In a medium bowl, combine eggs and brown sugar. Stir in remaining 1/3 cup flour, baking powder, salt, vanilla and lemon juice. Fold in chopped walnuts and chopped apricots. If desired, stir in shredded coconut. Pour mixture over prepared crust. Bake in oven for an additional 20 minutes, until firm. Let cool and dust with powdered sugar before cutting into bars.

Chewy Chocolate Peanut Bars

Makes 4 dozen

1 C. corn syrup	**1 tsp. vanilla**
3/4 C. peanut butter	**2 1/4 C. quick cooking oats**
1 1/2 C. chocolate chips	**1 3/4 C. unsalted peanuts**

In a medium saucepan over medium heat, combine corn syrup, peanut butter and chocolate chips. Bring to a boil, stirring constantly. Continue to boil for 5 minutes. Remove from heat and stir in vanilla, oats and peanuts. Pour mixture into a well greased 10x15" jelly roll pan. When slightly cooled, grease hands and pat down mixture in pan. Chill in refrigerator up to 8 hours and let stand for 20 minutes before cutting into bars.

Raspberry Oat Bars

Makes 2 dozen

3/4 C. butter, softened
1 C. brown sugar
1 1/2 C. rolled oats
1 1/2 C. flour

1 tsp. salt
1/2 tsp. baking powder
1 (10 oz.) jar raspberry
    preserves

    Preheat oven to 400°. Grease a 9x13" baking dish and set aside. In a large bowl, cream together butter and brown sugar, mixing until smooth. In a separate bowl, combine rolled oats, flour, salt and baking powder. Stir oats mixture into butter mixture and mix until well combined. Press half of the mixture into the bottom of prepared baking dish. Spread raspberry preserves over crust. Crumble remaining crust mixture over raspberry preserves. Bake in oven for 20 to 25 minutes or until bars are light brown. Remove from oven and let cool completely before cutting into bars.

Almond-Raspberry Meringue Bars

Makes 3 dozen

1 C. butter, softened	2 C. flour
7 oz. almond paste	3/4 C. seedless raspberry jam
1/2 C. brown sugar	3 egg whites
1 egg	1/2 C. sugar
1/2 tsp. almond extract	1/2 C. shredded coconut

Preheat oven to 350°. Line a 9x13" baking dish with aluminum foil and lightly grease the aluminum foil. To make crust, in a large bowl, combine butter, almond paste and brown sugar, mixing until smooth. Beat in egg and almond extract. Mix in flour and stir until well blended. Pat mixture into prepared baking dish. Bake in oven for 20 to 25 minutes or until golden brown. Let cool slightly and spread raspberry jam over crust. In a medium mixing bowl, beat egg whites until soft peaks form. Gradually beat in sugar. Spread mixture over jam layer and sprinkle with shredded coconut. Bake in oven for an additional 15 to 20 minutes, until firm. Remove from oven and let cool on a wire rack before cutting into bars.

Apple Pie Slices

Makes 20 bars

2 1/2 C. flour	9 apples, peeled, cored
3/4 C. plus 2 T. sugar, divided	and sliced
1/2 tsp. salt	1/2 tsp. cinnamon
2 eggs, separated	1 1/2 C. powdered sugar
1/2 C. plus 3 T. milk, divided	Pinch of salt
1 C. shortening	1 tsp. vanilla

Preheat oven to 350°. Grease and flour a 9x13" baking dish and set aside. In a medium bowl, combine flour, 2 tablespoons sugar and 1/2 teaspoon salt. Cut in shortening until mixture resembles coarse crumbs. In a small bowl, combine egg yolks and 1/2 cup milk. On a lightly floured flat surface, roll half of the dough into a 9x13" rectangle. Transfer rolled dough to prepared baking sheet. Brush a light coating of egg whites onto dough. Fill with sliced apples. Sprinkle remaining 3/4 cup sugar and cinnamon over apples. Roll out remaining dough and place over apples in baking dish. Brush top layer of dough lightly with egg whites. Bake in oven for 35 to 40 minutes, until crust is golden. In a small bowl, combine powdered sugar, a pinch of salt, vanilla and remaining 3 tablespoons milk, mixing until smooth. Drizzle glaze over cooled crust and cut into bars.

Berry Crumb Bars

Makes 12 to 15 bars

1 C. sugar	Pinch of salt
1 tsp. baking powder	Pinch of cinnamon
3 C. flour	4 C. raspberries
1 C. shortening	1/2 C. sugar
1 egg	3 tsp. cornstarch

Preheat oven to 375°. Grease a 9x13" baking dish and set aside. In a medium bowl, combine sugar, baking powder, flour, shortening, egg, salt and cinnamon and mix well. Dough should be crumbly. Pat half of the dough into the bottom of the prepared pan. In a separate bowl, combine raspberries, sugar and cornstarch. Place raspberry mixture over crust in pan. Crumble remaining half of the dough mixture over raspberries. Bake in oven for 45 minutes or until topping is lightly browned.

Cranberry Bars

Makes 2 dozen

1 (12 oz.) pkg. whole
   cranberries
1 C. sugar
3/4 C. water
1 (18 1/4 oz.) pkg. yellow
   cake mix

3/4 C. butter, melted
2 eggs
1 C. rolled oats
3/4 C. brown sugar
1 tsp. ground ginger
1 tsp. cinnamon

In a medium saucepan over medium heat, combine cranberries, sugar and water. Cook for about 15 minutes, stirring occasionally, until cranberries pop and mixture has thickened. Remove from heat and let cool. Preheat oven to 350°. In a large bowl, combine yellow cake mix, melted butter and eggs. Stir in oats, brown sugar, ground ginger and cinnamon. Set aside 1 1/2 cups of the oats mixture. Press remaining mixture into the bottom of a 9x13" baking dish, pressing down evenly. Spread cooled cranberry mixture over crust. Pinch remaining oats mixture into crumbs and sprinkle evenly over cranberry mixture. Bake in oven for 35 to 40 minutes or until topping is lightly browned. Remove from oven and let cool in pan for about 40 minutes before cutting into bars.

Cakes

Red Hat Chocolate Cake

Makes 8 to 10 servings

2 C. flour	3 eggs
3/4 C. cocoa powder	1 T. plus 2 tsp. vanilla, divided
1 tsp. baking soda	1 1/2 C. plus 1/3 C. milk, divided
3/4 tsp. baking powder	4 C. powdered sugar
1/2 tsp. salt	Drops of red food coloring
1 1/4 C. butter, softened, divided	1 pint fresh raspberries
2 C. sugar	

Preheat oven to 350°. Lightly grease and flour the bottoms and sides of three 8" round pans. Line the bottoms of the pans with waxed paper and set aside. In a medium bowl, combine flour, cocoa powder, baking soda, baking powder and salt. In a large mixing bowl, beat 3/4 cup butter at medium high speed for 30 seconds. Gradually add sugar, 1/4 cup at a time, beating for 3 to 4 minutes, until combined. Scrape sides of bowl and beat for an additional 2 minutes. Add eggs, one at a time, beating well after each addition. Add 2 teaspoons vanilla. Alternating, add flour mixture and 1 1/2 cups milk, beating at low speed just until combined. Beat at medium high speed for 20 seconds. Pour batter evenly into prepared pans. Bake in oven for 30 to 35 minutes or until a toothpick inserted in center of cakes comes out clean. Let cakes cool in pans for 10 minutes before removing to a wire rack. To prepare frosting, in a medium bowl, cream remaining 1/2 cup butter. Alternating, add powdered sugar and remaining 1/3 cup milk. Mix in remaining 1 tablespoon vanilla and add food coloring to reach desired shade of red. Frosting should be thin, but not watery. Assemble cake by spreading frosting between cake layers and finally over entire top of cake and sides. Garnish with fresh raspberries.

Glazed Carrot Cake

Makes 10 servings

1 1/2 C. flour	3 medium carrots, finely
1 C. sugar	shredded
1 1/2 C. baking soda	1 C. shredded coconut
1 tsp. cinnamon	1 C. powdered sugar
1/2 tsp. salt	1 (3 oz.) pkg. cream cheese,
3/4 C. vegetable oil	softened
2 eggs, slightly beaten	1 T. grated orange peel
1 tsp. vanilla	1 T. orange juice

Preheat oven to 350°. In a large bowl, combine flour, sugar, baking soda, cinnamon and salt. Stir in vegetable oil, eggs and vanilla and mix well. Gently fold in shredded carrots and shredded coconut. The batter should be thick. Spread batter into a greased and flour 9" round pan. Bake in oven for 40 to 45 minutes or until a toothpick inserted in center of cake comes out clean. Meanwhile, in a small mixing bowl, beat together powdered sugar, cream cheese, grated orange peel and orange juice at low speed until smooth. Pour frosting over warm cake.

Chocolate Rocky Road Cake

Makes 15 servings

2 C. flour	2 C. miniature marshmallows
1 1/2 C. sugar	1 (3 oz.) pkg. cream cheese,
1/2 C. cocoa powder	softened
3/4 C. butter, softened, divided	1 (1 oz.) square baking
1 C. water	chocolate
3 eggs	2 T. milk
1 1/4 tsp. baking powder	3 C. powdered sugar
1 tsp. baking soda	1/2 C. coarsely chopped peanuts
2 tsp. vanilla, divided	

Preheat oven to 350°. In a large mixing bowl, combine flour, sugar, cocoa powder, 1/2 cup butter, water, eggs, baking powder, baking soda and 1 teaspoon vanilla. Beat at low speed, scraping bowl often, just until moistened. Beat at high speed for 1 to 2 minutes, until batter is smooth. Pour batter into a greased and floured 9x13" baking dish. Bake in oven for 30 to 40 minutes or until a toothpick inserted in center of cake comes out clean. Remove from oven and sprinkle marshmallows over warm cake. Return to oven for 2 minutes, until marshmallows are softened. Meanwhile, in a medium saucepan over medium heat, combine remaining 1/4 cup butter, cream cheese, baking chocolate and milk. Cook for 8 to 10 minutes, stirring occasionally, until melted. Remove from heat and stir in powdered sugar and remaining 1 teaspoon vanilla. Pour mixture over marshmallows on cake and swirl topping together. Sprinkle chopped peanuts over topping.

Lemon Poppy Seed Pound Cake

Makes 16 servings

3 C. flour	1/2 tsp. baking powder
2 C. sugar	1/2 tsp. salt
1/4 C. poppy seeds	4 tsp. grated lemon peel
1 C. butter, softened	1/2 tsp. vanilla
1 C. buttermilk	1 C. powdered sugar
4 eggs	1 to 2 T. lemon juice
1/2 tsp. baking soda	

Preheat oven to 325°. In a large mixing bowl, combine flour, sugar, poppy seeds, butter, buttermilk, eggs, baking soda, baking powder, salt and grated lemon peel. Beat at low speed until moistened. Beat at high speed, for 1 to 2 minutes, until batter is smooth. Pour batter into a greased and floured bundt pan or 10" tube pan. Bake for 55 to 65 minutes or until a toothpick inserted in center of cake comes out clean. Let cool for 10 minutes before removing from pan. In a small bowl, combine powdered sugar and lemon juice, mixing until smooth. Drizzle glaze over cooled cake.

Legendary
Honey Cake

Makes 12 servings

3 T. sliced almonds	1/2 C. honey
5 large eggs, separated	1/4 C. strong brewed coffee
3/4 C. sugar	Grated peel of 1 lemon
2 C. flour	2 tsp. lemon juice
1/2 tsp. baking powder	1 T. Scotch or Irish whiskey
1/2 tsp. baking soda	Pinch of salt

Preheat oven to 325°. Lightly grease a 9" tube pan or bundt pan. Sprinkle sliced almonds across bottom of pan and set aside. In a medium mixing bowl, beat egg yolks and sugar for 5 to 7 minutes at medium high speed until thickened. Into a separate bowl, sift flour, baking powder and baking soda. In a large bowl, whisk together honey and coffee. Gradually whisk in egg yolk mixture. Add lemon zest, lemon juice and whiskey. Gently fold in flour mixture in 3 batches. In a separate mixing bowl, beat egg whites and salt until stiff peaks form. Fold beaten egg whites into batter. Pour batter over almonds in prepared pan. Bake in oven for about 45 minutes or until cake springs back when gently pressed. Let cool on a wire rack before serving.

Lightning Cake

Makes 6 servings

1 C. flour
1 tsp. baking powder
1/2 C. butter, softened
1 C. plus 1 T. sugar, divided
4 large eggs

Grated peel and juice of
   1/2 lemon
1/4 C. chopped almonds
Powdered sugar, for garnish

Preheat oven to 350°. Grease and flour an 8" round pan and set aside. In a medium bowl, combine flour and baking powder and set aside. In a medium mixing bowl, beat together butter and 1 cup sugar at medium high speed until lightened. Beat in eggs, one at a time, and add grated lemon peel and lemon juice. Reduce speed to low and add flour mixture, beating just until combined. Pour batter into prepared pan. In a small bowl, combine chopped almonds and remaining 1 tablespoons sugar. Sprinkle chopped almond mixture over batter. Bake in oven about 26 minutes or until a toothpick inserted in center of cake comes out clean. Remove from oven and let cool on a wire rack. Sprinkle top of cake with powdered sugar.

Chocolate Mocha Cheesecake

Makes 12 servings

1 1/3 C. graham cracker crumbs	3 eggs
1/4 C. plus 3 T. butter, melted	1 T. vanilla
1 C. plus 2 T. sugar, divided	1 to 2 tsp. instant coffee
1/2 C. sour cream	1 T. warm water
3 (8 oz.) pkgs. cream cheese, softened	1/4 C. cocoa powder
3 T. flour	2 (1.4 oz.) chocolate English toffee bars, chopped

Preheat oven to 325°. In a medium bowl, combine graham cracker crumbs, 1/4 cup melted butter and 2 tablespoons sugar. Mix well and press mixture evenly onto the bottom of a 9" springform pan. Bake in oven for 10 minutes and let cool. In a large mixing bowl, combine 3/4 cup sugar, sour cream, cream cheese and flour. Beat at medium speed for 2 to 3 minutes, until smooth and creamy. Add eggs and vanilla. In a small bowl, combine coffee and warm water, mixing until coffee is dissolved. Mix in 1 cup of the cream cheese mixture and set aside. Add remaining 1/4 cup sugar, cocoa powder and remaining 3 tablespoons melted butter to cream cheese mixture. Pour cream cheese mixture into crust. Pour coffee mixture over cream cheese mixture in crust. For a marbled effect, pull knife through cheesecake filling. Bake in oven for 50 to 70 minutes or until center of cake is set. Turn off oven, leaving cheesecake in oven for 2 hours. Remove from oven and chill in refrigerator for 8 hours or overnight. Before serving, sprinkle chopped English toffee bars over cheesecake.

Buttery Coconut Pecan Cake

Makes 15 servings

2 1/4 C. flour
1 1/2 C. sugar
1 1/3 C. butter, softened,
    divided
1 C. buttermilk
4 eggs
1 tsp. baking soda

1/2 tsp. salt
1 T. plus 1 1/2 tsp. vanilla,
    divided
1 C. shredded coconut
1 C. chopped pecans
3 C. powdered sugar
1 to 3 T. milk

Preheat oven to 350°. In a large mixing bowl, combine flour, sugar, 1 cup butter, buttermilk, eggs, baking soda, salt and 1 tablespoon vanilla. Beat at low speed, scraping bowl often, until ingredients are moistened. Beat at high speed for 3 to 4 minutes, until smooth. Fold in shredded coconut and chopped pecans by hand. Pour batter into a greased and floured 9x13" baking dish. Bake in oven for 45 to 50 minutes or until center of cake is firm. Remove from oven and let cool on a wire rack. In a 1-quart saucepan over medium heat, melt remaining 1/3 cup butter until lightly browned. In a small mixing bowl, combine melted butter, powdered sugar and remaining 1 1/2 teaspoons vanilla. Beat at medium speed and gradually add milk until frosting is smooth and spreadable. Spread frosting over cooled cake.

Grandma's Banana Cake

Makes 8 to 10 servings

2 1/4 C. cake flour	2 tsp. vanilla
1 1/2 tsp. baking powder	3/4 C. very ripe mashed
1 1/2 tsp. baking soda	bananas
1/4 tsp. salt	1/4 C. plus 2 T. sour cream
3/4 C. butter, softened	or plain yogurt
1 1/2 C. sugar	Powdered sugar, optional
3 large eggs	

Preheat oven to 350°. Generously grease and flour a bundt pan or 10" tube pan. Into a medium bowl, sift cake flour, baking powder, baking soda and salt. In a medium mixing bowl, beat butter at medium high speed until lightened. Gradually add sugar and beat until fluffy. Beat in eggs, one at a time, mixing well after each addition. Mix in vanilla. Reduce speed to low and, alternating, add flour mixture and mashed bananas in batches. Mix in sour cream, being careful not to over mix. Pour batter into prepared pan. Bake in oven for 50 to 55 minutes or until a toothpick inserted in center of cake comes out clean. Remove from oven and let cool in pan for 10 to 15 minutes before turning out onto a wire rack. If desired, sprinkle powdered sugar over cooled cake.

Choco-Butterscotch Cake

Makes 20 servings

2 1/2 C. flour
1 1/2 C. sugar
3/4 C. butter, softened
1 1/4 C. cold water
3 eggs
2 (1 oz.) squares baking chocolate, melted

1 tsp. baking soda
1 tsp. salt
1 tsp. vanilla
1 C. butterscotch chips
1/2 C. chopped walnuts

Preheat oven to 350°. In a large mixing bowl, combine flour, sugar, butter, cold water, eggs, melted chocolate, baking soda, salt and vanilla. Beat at low speed until moistened. Increase speed to medium and beat for 2 minutes, until well mixed. Spread batter into a greased 9x13" baking dish. Sprinkle butterscotch chips and chopped walnuts over batter. Bake in oven for 40 to 45 minutes or until cake springs back when gently pressed. Remove from oven and let cool on a wire rack.

Walnut Spice Cake

Makes 12 servings

2 C. flour
1 1/3 C. sugar
2 tsp. baking powder
1 tsp. salt
1/4 tsp. baking soda
1 tsp. cinnamon
1/2 tsp. nutmeg
1/2 C. butter, softened

1/2 C. frozen orange juice
    concentrate, thawed
1/2 C. milk
2 eggs
2 C. whipped topping
1 C. chopped walnuts
12 walnut halves
12 fresh orange sections

Preheat oven to 350°. In a large mixing bowl, combine flour, sugar, baking powder, salt, baking soda, cinnamon, nutmeg, butter, orange juice concentrate and milk. Beat at low speed for 2 minutes. Add eggs and beat for an additional 2 minutes. Pour batter into two greased and floured 8" cake pans. Bake in oven for 30 to 35 minutes or until a toothpick inserted in center of cakes comes out clean. Remove cakes from oven and let cool on a wire rack. Place one cake on a serving plate. Spread 1/3 of the whipped cream over cake and top with the other cake. Cover tops and sides of cake evenly with remaining whipped cream. Press chopped walnuts into sides of cake. Garnish top of cake with walnut halves and orange sections. Refrigerate cake until ready to serve.

Boston Cream Cake

Makes 12 servings

2 T. flour	1 C. milk, divided
1 1/2 C. cake flour	3/4 C. light cream, divided
2 tsp. baking powder	Pinch of salt
1/4 tsp. salt	4 tsp. cornstarch
8 T. butter, softened, divided	3 (1 oz.) squares semi-sweet
1 C. sugar, divided	baking chocolate
4 eggs, divided	1/2 C. powdered sugar
2 tsp. vanilla, divided	

Preheat oven to 375°. Grease and flour two 9" round pans. Into a medium bowl, sift flour, cake flour, baking powder and salt. In a large mixing bowl, cream together 6 tablespoons butter and 3/4 cup sugar until lightened. Beat in 2 eggs, one at a time and add 1 teaspoon vanilla. Alternating, add flour mixture and 1/2 cup milk, beating well after each addition. Pour batter evenly into prepared pans. Bake in oven for 15 minutes or until a toothpick inserted in center of cakes comes out clean. To make filling, in a medium saucepan over medium heat, combine 1/2 cup light cream and 1/4 cup milk. Cook until bubbles form around edge of saucepan and immediately add remaining 1/4 cup sugar. Remove from heat. In a small bowl, combine remaining 1/4 cup milk and hot cream mixture, whisking constantly. Return to saucepan over low heat and bring to a boil, stirring constantly, until thickened and smooth. Remove from heat and stir in 1/2 teaspoon vanilla and set aside. In a heavy saucepan over low heat, combine baking chocolate and remaining 2 tablespoons butter, mixing until melted. Remove from heat and add remaining 1/4 cup light cream, whisking constantly. When mixture is smooth, add powdered sugar and remaining 1/2 teaspoon vanilla and beat vigorously until smooth. Spread cooled cream mixture over 1 of the cakes. Top with other cake and pour chocolate frosting over top of cake, allowing frosting to spill down sides of cake.

Angel Food Cake

Makes 16 servings

1 1/2 C. egg whites
1 tsp. cream of tartar
1/2 tsp. vanilla
1/2 tsp. almond extract

1 1/4 C. cake flour
1 3/4 C. sugar
1/4 tsp. salt

In a medium mixing bowl, beat egg whites until stiff peaks form and stir in cream of tartar, vanilla and almond extract. Into a medium bowl, sift cake flour, sugar and salt. Sift dry ingredients 5 times. Gently combine egg whites and dry ingredients and pour batter into an ungreased 10" tube pan. Place cake pan in cold oven and heat oven to 325°. Cook for 1 hour or until cake is golden brown. Remove cake from oven and invert, allowing cake to cool in pan. When cake is cooled, remove from pan.

Blueberry Coffee Cake

Makes 12 servings

1 C. brown sugar	1 tsp. vanilla
2 2/3 C. flour, divided	2 tsp. baking powder
1 tsp. cinnamon	1/2 tsp. salt
1 C. butter, divided	1/2 C. milk
1 C. sugar	1 C. blueberries
1 egg	1/4 C. powdered sugar

Preheat oven to 350°. Grease a bundt pan and set aside. In a small bowl, combine brown sugar, 2/3 cup flour and cinnamon. Using a pastry blender, cut in 1/2 cup butter until mixture is crumbly. Set aside. In a large mixing bowl, beat remaining 1/2 cup butter until creamy. Add sugar, beating until fluffy. Add egg and vanilla. In a separate bowl, combine remaining 2 cups flour, baking powder and salt. Alternating, add flour mixture and milk to butter mixture, beating well after each addition. Spread half of the batter into prepared pan. Cover with blueberries and pour remaining half of batter over blueberries. Sprinkle crumbly mixture over batter. Bake in oven for 55 to 60 minutes or until cake is golden brown. Remove pan to a wire rack to cool. Once cake has cooled, invert onto wire rack and dust with powdered sugar.

Buttery Cinnamon Cake

Makes 14 servings

2 C. flour
1 T. baking powder
1 3/4 tsp. cinnamon, divided
3/4 tsp. salt
2/3 C. shortening
1 1/3 C. plus 1/2 C. sugar, divided

2 1/2 tsp. vanilla, divided
3 eggs
2/3 C. milk
6 T. butter, softened
1/3 C. water

Preheat oven to 350°. Grease and lightly flour a 10" bundt pan and set aside. In a medium bowl, combine flour, baking powder, 1 teaspoon cinnamon and salt. Set aside. In a large mixing bowl, combine shortening, 1 1/3 cups sugar and 1 1/2 teaspoons vanilla, beating until lightened and fluffy. Add eggs, one at a time, beating well after each addition. Alternating, add flour mixture and milk to shortening mixture. Beat well and pour batter into prepared pan. Bake in oven for 40 to 45 minutes or until a toothpick inserted in center of cake comes out clean. Meanwhile, in a medium saucepan over medium heat, combine remaining 1/2 cup sugar, butter, water, remaining 1 teaspoon vanilla and remaining 3/4 teaspoon cinnamon. Heat, stirring frequently, until melted. Remove cake from oven and poke holes around top of cake with a fork. Pour warm cinnamon mixture into holes and onto top and sides of cake.

Blue Ribbon White Cake

Makes 12 servings

5 T. cornstarch	1/4 tsp. cream of tartar
2 1/2 C. flour	1 1/2 C. sugar
3 1/2 tsp. baking powder	6 T. butter
1 tsp. salt	2 tsp. grated orange peel
2/3 C. vegetable oil	1/4 tsp. salt
1/2 C. milk	4 C. powdered sugar, sifted
3/4 C. water	1/2 C. fresh orange juice
1 T. vanilla	1 T. fresh lemon juice
4 egg whites	

Preheat oven to 350°. Grease and line two 9" round pans with parchment paper. Grease and flour the paper. Into a medium bowl, sift cornstarch, flour, baking powder and salt. Add vegetable oil, milk, water and vanilla and beat until smooth. In a medium mixing bowl, beat egg whites until frothy. Add cream of tartar and beat until stiff peaks form. Gradually add sugar and beat until well blended. Fold egg whites mixture into batter and pour batter into prepared pans. Bake in oven for 35 to 40 minutes. Remove from oven and let cool on a wire rack. Meanwhile, to prepare frosting, in a medium mixing bowl, beat butter until lightened and fluffy. Add grated orange peel and salt. Alternating, add powdered sugar and orange and lemon juices. Mix well and spread over cooled cake.

Apricot Brandy Cake

Makes 16 servings

1/2 C. chopped pecans
1 (18 1/4 oz.) pkg. yellow cake mix
1 (3.4 oz.) pkg. instant vanilla pudding mix
1/2 C. plus 2 T. apricot brandy, divided
1/2 C. vegetable oil
1/2 C. plus 2 T. water, divided
4 eggs
1/4 C. butter
1 C. powdered sugar

Preheat oven to 350°. Grease and flour a 10" bundt pan and sprinkle chopped pecans evenly over bottom of pan. In a large mixing bowl, combine yellow cake mix, vanilla pudding mix, 1/2 cup apricot brandy, vegetable oil, 1/2 cup water and eggs. Beat at medium speed for 10 minutes and pour batter into prepared pan. Bake in oven for 50 to 55 minutes or until a toothpick inserted in center of cake comes out clean. Remove from oven and let cake cool in pan for 10 minutes before turning out onto a wire rack. To make glaze, in a medium saucepan over medium heat, combine butter, remaining 2 tablespoons apricot brandy and remaining 2 tablespoons water. Bring to a boil and let simmer for 5 minutes. Remove from heat and let cool slightly. Stir in powdered sugar until glaze reaches desired consistency. Drizzle glaze over cooled cake.

Caramel Cake

Makes 24 servings

3 C. sifted cake flour	3/4 C. butter
3 tsp. baking powder	3 eggs
1/2 tsp. salt	1 tsp. vanilla
1 3/4 C. sugar, divided	2/3 C. milk
1/3 C. hot water	

Preheat oven to 350°. Line two 9" round pans with parchment paper. Into a medium bowl, sift cake flour, baking powder and salt. Sift dry ingredients 3 times and set aside. In a heavy skillet over medium heat, combine 1/2 cup sugar, stirring constantly, until sugar melts. Continue cooking until sugar becomes dark brown and remove from heat. Slowly add hot water, stirring until dissolved. In a large bowl, cream together butter and remaining 1 1/4 cups sugar until lightened and fluffy. Add eggs, one at a time, beating well after each addition. Add vanilla and 3 tablespoons dark sugar mixture. Alternating, add sifted flour mixture and milk to butter mixture. Pour batter into prepared pans and bake for 25 to 30 minutes or until a toothpick inserted in center of cake comes out clean.

Chocolate Chip Cookie Ice Cream Cake

Makes 12 servings

1 (18 oz.) pkg. small chocolate chip cookies
1/4 C. margarine, melted
1 C. hot fudge topping, divided
2 qts. vanilla ice cream, softened
1 C. whipped cream
12 cherries

Crush half of the small chocolate chip cookies into crumbs. In a medium bowl, combine crushed cookies and melted butter and press mixture onto the bottom of a 9" springform pan or pie plate. Stand remaining whole cookies around the edge of pan. Spread 3/4 cup fudge topping over crust and place in freezer for 15 minutes. Meanwhile, softened 1 quart ice cream in microwave or on countertop. After crust has chilled, spread softened ice cream evenly over fudge layer. Return to freezer for 30 minutes. Scoop remaining 1 quart ice cream into balls and arrange balls over ice cream layer. Freeze for 4 hours or overnight, until firm. Before serving, garnish cake with remaining 1/4 cup fudge topping, whipped cream and cherries.

Pies & Pastries

Yummy Peaches & Cream Pie

Makes 8 servings

3/4 C. flour
1/2 tsp. salt
1 tsp. baking powder
1 (4 serving size) pkg. non-instant vanilla pudding mix
3 T. butter, softened
1 egg

1/2 C. milk
1 (29 oz.) can sliced peaches, drained, syrup reserved
1 (8 oz.) pkg. cream cheese, softened
1/2 C. plus 1 T. sugar, divided
1 tsp. cinnamon

Preheat oven to 350°. Grease the bottom and sides of a deep 10" pie pan. In a medium mixing bowl, combine flour, salt, baking powder and vanilla pudding mix. Add butter, egg and milk. Beat at medium speed for 2 minutes. Pour mixture into prepared pie pan. Arrange peach slices over mixture in pan. In a small mixing bowl, beat cream cheese at medium low speed until fluffy. Add 1/2 cup sugar and 3 tablespoons reserved peach syrup. Beat for 2 minutes and pour over peaches in pan, covering to within 1" from sides of pan. In a small bowl, combine remaining 1 tablespoon sugar and cinnamon. Sprinkle mixture over top of ingredients in pan. Bake in oven for 30 to 35 minutes, or until crust of pie is golden brown. Chill in refrigerator before serving.

Layered Lemon and Fruit Pie

Makes 8 servings

1 (21 oz.) can cherry or
   blueberry pie filling
1 (9") prepared graham
   cracker pie crust
1 (8 oz.) pkg. cream cheese,
   softened

1 C. cold milk
1 (4 serving size) pkg. instant
   lemon pudding mix
1 (8 oz.) container frozen
   whipped topping,
   thawed, divided

Spread half of the pie filling over bottom of pie crust. In a large bowl, beat cream cheese with a wire whisk until smooth. Gradually beat in milk until well blended. Add pudding mix and beat until smooth. Gently fold in half of the whipped topping. Spread mixture over pie filling in crust. Spread remaining whipping topping over cream cheese mixture in pie crust. Chill in refrigerator for 3 hours before serving.

Autumn Apple Pie

Makes 8 servings

6 C. thinly sliced apples	**1/4 tsp. nutmeg**
Juice of 1 lemon	**3 T. flour**
1/2 C. brown sugar	**1/4 C. butter, chilled and diced**
1/2 C. plus 1 T. sugar, divided	**9 caramel squares, quartered**
2 tsp. cinnamon	**1 (9") double crust pie pastry**

Preheat oven to 375°. In a large bowl, combine apples slices, lemon juice, brown sugar, 1/2 cup sugar, cinnamon, nutmeg, flour, butter and caramel squares. Stir until apples are evenly coated. Line a 9" pie pan with one of the pie pastry crusts. Spoon filling into pie crust and top with remaining pie pastry crust. Trim and seal the edges. Place pie on a baking sheet covered with aluminum foil. Poke holes in top pie pastry crust. Sprinkle top of crust lightly with remaining 1 tablespoon sugar. Bake in oven for 50 minutes. If overflowing occurs after 30 minutes, reduce oven temperature to 350°. Serve warm.

Old Fashioned Raisin Pie

Makes 8 servings

2 C. raisins	1/4 tsp. salt
2 C. water	1 T. white vinegar
1/2 C. brown sugar	1 T. butter or margarine
2 T. cornstarch	1 (9") double crust pie pastry
1/2 tsp. cinnamon	

Preheat oven to 425°. In a small saucepan over medium heat, combine raisins and water. Bring to a boil for 5 minutes. In a small bowl, combine brown sugar, cornstarch, cinnamon and salt. Add brown sugar mixture to raisins. Cook, stirring often, until syrup is clear. Remove from heat and stir in vinegar and butter. Mix well and let cool slightly. Line a 9" pie pan with one of the pie pastry crusts. Spoon raisin filling into pie crust and top with remaining pie pastry crust. Trim and seal the edges. Place pie on a baking sheet covered with aluminum foil. Poke holes in top pie pastry crust. Bake in oven for 30 to 35 minutes.

Chocolate Covered Banana Cream Pie

Makes 8 servings

3 C. crushed vanilla wafers
1/2 C. chopped pecans
2/3 C. butter, melted
2 C. chocolate chips
4 C. milk, divided
4 1/2 C. miniature marshmallows, divided

2 large bananas, sliced
2 (4 serving size each) pkgs. instant vanilla pudding mix
1 C. frozen whipped topping, thawed
1 (1 1/2 oz.) milk chocolate candy bar, grated

Preheat oven to 375°. In a medium bowl, combine crushed vanilla wafers, chopped pecans and melted butter. Press mixture into the bottom of a 9x13" baking dish. Bake in oven for 5 minutes. Remove from oven and let cool. In a medium saucepan over low heat, combine chocolate chips, 1 cup milk and 2 cups marshmallows. Cook, stirring frequently, until mixture is melted. Pour mixture over cooled crust in pan. Chill in refrigerator for 1 hour. Arrange banana slices over chilled chocolate layer. Prepare pudding according to package instructions, using remaining 3 cups milk. Fold in whipped topping and remaining 2 1/2 cups marshmallows. Pour mixture over bananas in pan. Sprinkle grated chocolate over pudding layer in pan. Chill in refrigerator for 2 to 3 hours before serving.

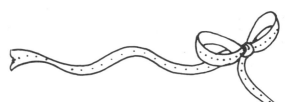

Creamy Pear Pie

Makes 8 servings

1/3 C. sugar	1/2 tsp. lemon extract
1/4 C. plus 2 T. flour, divided	1/2 tsp. almond extract
4 C. peeled and sliced pears	1 (9") unbaked pie crust
1 C. sour cream	2 T. brown sugar
1/2 tsp. vanilla	2 T. butter or margarine, melted

Preheat oven to 400°. In a large bowl, combine sugar and 2 tablespoons flour. Add sliced pears and toss until evenly coated. Stir in sour cream, vanilla, lemon extract and almond extract. Pour mixture into unbaked pie crust. In a small bowl, combine remaining 1/4 cup flour and brown sugar. Add melted butter and mix with fingers until mixture is crumbly. Sprinkle mixture evenly over filling in pie crust. Bake in oven for 10 minutes. Reduce oven temperature to 350° and bake for an additional 45 minutes, or until pears are tender.

Raspberry Pie

Makes 8 servings

4 C. raspberries	1/8 tsp. salt
1 C. sugar	4 tsp. butter
2 1/2 T. tapioca	1 (9" or 10") single crust
1 T. lemon juice	pie pastry
1/4 tsp. cinnamon	1 T. half n' half

Preheat oven to 425°. In a medium bowl, combine raspberries, sugar, tapioca, lemon juice, cinnamon and salt, mixing until raspberries are evenly coated. Pour raspberry mixture into a 9" or 10" pie pan. Dot with butter and top with pie pastry crust. Cut slits in top crust and brush with half n' half. Bake in oven for 15 minutes. Reduce oven temperature to 375° and bake for an additional 25 minutes.

Margarita Party Pie

Makes 8 servings

1 1/2 C. crushed pretzels	**1/4 C. tequila**
1/4 C. sugar	**4 T. orange-flavored liqueur**
2/3 C. butter, melted	**1 C. fresh sliced strawberries**
1 (14 oz.) can sweetened	**2 drops red food coloring**
condensed milk	**2 drops yellow food coloring**
1/4 C. fresh lime juice	**2 C. whipped topping, divided**

In a large bowl, combine crushed pretzels, sugar and melted butter. Mix well and press into the bottom of a 9" pie pan. In a large bowl, combine sweetened condensed milk, lime juice, tequila and orange-flavored liqueur. Pour half of the mixture into a separate bowl. To one of the bowls, add sliced strawberries and red food coloring. To the other bowl, add yellow food coloring. Fold 1 cup whipped topping into each bowl. Alternating, spoon mixtures into crust to makes layers of red and yellow filling. Place in freezer for 4 hours or overnight.

Strawberry Daiquiri Pie

Makes 2 pies or 16 servings

1 (10 oz.) can frozen
strawberry daiquiri mixer
1 C. sweetened condensed milk
1 (8 oz.) container frozen
whipped topping, thawed

1 (10 oz.) pkg. frozen
strawberries, thawed
2 (9") prepared graham
crackers crusts

In a large bowl, combine daiquiri mixer, sweetened condensed milk and whipped topping. Stir until mixture is smooth and creamy. Add thawed strawberries and blend into mixture. Fill pie crusts with mixture and chill in refrigerator for 4 hours or place in freezer until set.

All American Apple Pie

Makes 8 servings

2 C. plus 3 T. flour, divided	1 tsp. salt
1/2 C. vegetable oil	6 Fuji apples, cored and sliced
2 T. cold milk	3/4 tsp. cinnamon
1 1/4 C. plus 1 1/2 tsp. sugar, divided	1/2 tsp. nutmeg
	1/2 C. butter, melted

Preheat oven to 350°. To make crust, in a large bowl, combine 1 1/2 cups flour, vegetable oil, milk, 1 1/2 teaspoons sugar and salt, mixing until evenly blended. Press mixture evenly into bottom and up sides a 9" pie pan. Crimp edges of dough. To make filling, in a medium bowl, combine 3/4 cup sugar, 3 tablespoons flour, cinnamon and nutmeg. Add sliced apples and mix until apples are evenly coated. Spread mixture evenly into pie crust in pan. Using a pastry blender, in a small bowl, combine remaining 1/2 cup flour, remaining 1/2 cup sugar and butter, stirring until mixture is crumbly. Sprinkle over apples in pie crust. Place pie on a baking sheet covered with aluminum foil. Bake in oven for 45 minutes.

Blueberry Cheesecake Pie

Makes 6 servings

1 1/2 C. graham cracker crumbs	2 eggs
6 T. butter, melted	1 qt. fresh blueberries
2 C. sugar, divided	1/2 C. water
1 (8 oz.) pkg. cream cheese, softened	3 T. cornstarch
	1 (16 oz.) pkg. frozen whipped topping, thawed

Preheat oven to 350°. In a medium bowl, combine graham cracker crumbs, melted butter and 1/2 cup sugar. Press mixture into the bottom of an 8x12" baking dish. In a large mixing bowl, combine cream cheese, eggs and 1/2 cup sugar, beating at medium speed until smooth. Spread cream cheese mixture over crust. Bake in oven for 15 minutes. To make filling, in a large saucepan over medium heat, combine blueberries, water, cornstarch and remaining 1 cup sugar. Cook, stirring often, until thickened. Spread blueberry filling over baked cream cheese layer in pan. Let cool. Spread whipped topping over cooled blueberry mixture. Chill in refrigerator for 4 hours or overnight before cutting into squares.

Strawberry Rhubarb Cream Pie

Makes 10 servings

1 1/2 C. sugar	**4 C. chopped rhubarb**
1/4 C. flour	**3 C. fresh halved strawberries**
3/4 tsp. nutmeg	**1 (9") double crust pie pastry**
3 eggs, beaten	**1 egg white**

Preheat oven to 400°. In a large bowl, combine sugar, flour and nutmeg. Stir in beaten eggs and fold in rhubarb until evenly coated. Add strawberries and mix until evenly incorporated. Line a 9" pie pan with one of the pie pastry crusts. Spoon rhubarb and strawberry filling into pie crust and top with remaining pie pastry crust. Trim and seal the edges. Place pie on a baking sheet covered with aluminum foil. Poke holes in top pie pastry crust and brush egg white over crust. Bake in oven for 50 to 60 minutes, until rhubarb is tender and crust is golden.

Danish Pastry Apple Bars

Makes 12 servings

2 1/2 C. flour	10 apples, peeled, cored
1 tsp. salt	and thinly sliced
1 C. shortening	1/2 C. brown sugar
1 egg, separated	1/4 C. sugar
1/2 C. milk	1/2 tsp. cinnamon
	1/4 tsp. nutmeg

Preheat oven to 375°. In a large bowl, combine flour and salt. Using a pastry blender, cut in shortening until mixture resembles coarse crumbs. In a measuring cup, beat egg yolk and add enough milk to make 2/3 cup liquid. Add egg yolk mixture to flour mixture, mixing until a damp dough forms. Divide dough in half. On a lightly floured surface, roll half of the dough into a rectangle and fit dough into a 9x13" baking dish. In a large bowl, combine apples slices, brown sugar, sugar, cinnamon and nutmeg. Pour apples mixture over crust in baking dish. Roll out remaining dough and place over apples in baking dish. Seal edges and cut slits in top of dough. Using a wire whisk, in a small bowl, beat egg white until frothy and brush over pastry crust. Bake in oven for 50 minutes, or until pastry is golden brown.

Pumpkin Pear Strudel

Makes 2 strudels or 10 servings

2 C. peeled, cored and
    diced pears
1 C. pumpkin puree
3/4 C. brown sugar
3/4 C. chopped walnuts
1/8 tsp. ground cloves

1/8 tsp. ground ginger
2 tsp. cinnamon, divided
1 (17 1/2 oz.) pkg. frozen
    puff pastry, thawed
1 large egg, beaten
1/4 C. sugar

Preheat oven to 375°. In a medium bowl, combine diced pears, pumpkin puree, brown sugar, chopped walnuts, ground cloves, ground ginger and 1 teaspoon cinnamon. Mix well. Lay 1 pastry sheet on a flat surface. Spoon half of the filling in a line across the center 1/3 of the pastry sheet. On either side of the filling, cut downward slanting strips, 3/4" thick, starting about 1" from top of pastry and sides of filling. Starting at top of pastry, fold left and right strips of pastry up and over filling, crossing strips to form a braided look. Press down on pastry to seal top and bottom of strudel. Place strudel on an ungreased jelly roll pan. Brush strudel with egg. In a small bowl, combine sugar and remaining 1 teaspoon cinnamon. Sprinkle mixture over strudel. Repeat with remaining 1 sheet pastry and remaining half of the filling. Bake in oven for 25 to 30 minutes, or until pastry is golden brown and puffy. Serve warm.

Cinnamon Pastries

Makes 18 servings

1 (8 oz.) pkg. cream cheese, softened	3 T. cinnamon
1 C. sugar, divided	18 slices bread, crusts removed
1 egg yolk	3/4 C. butter, melted

In a medium bowl, combine cream cheese, 1/4 cup sugar and egg yolk. In a small, shallow bowl, combine remaining 3/4 cup sugar and cinnamon. Spread 1 side of each slice of bread with cream cheese mixture. Roll bread slices into rolls, securing cream cheese filling inside. Dip rolls into melted butter and roll each pastry in cinnamon and sugar mixture. Arrange rolls pastries in a single layer on an ungreased baking sheet. Cover with aluminum foil and place in freezer at least 1 hour, until frozen. Preheat oven to 350°. Uncover frozen bread rolls and bake in oven for 25 minutes or until rolls are golden brown. Let cool slightly before serving.

White Chocolate Cranberry Pear Pastry

Makes 10 servings

1 (17 1/2 oz.) pkg. frozen puffy pastry, thawed	1 (6 oz.) pkg. white baking chocolate
1 egg, beaten	2 (15 oz.) can sliced pears, drained
1 T. water	1/4 C. dried cranberries

Preheat oven to 375°. In a small bowl, combine beaten egg and water. Unfold pastry sheets on a lightly floured flat surface and trim about 1" off the corner of each pastry sheet, reserving trimmings. Place 1 pastry on an ungreased baking sheet. Chop 4 squares of the white baking chocolate into small pieces. In a medium bowl, combine chopped white chocolate, pears and cranberries. Spread mixture into the center of pastry on baking sheet to within 1" of the edges of the pastry. Brush edges of pastry with water. Top with remaining pastry sheet, press edges together with a fork to seal. If desired, decorate pastry with reserved pastry trimmings. Brush egg mixture over pastry. Cut slits, 2" apart, in top pastry crust. Bake in oven for 35 minutes or until pastry is golden brown. Let cool for about 30 minutes on a wire rack. In a double boiler, melt remaining 2 squares white baking chocolate. Drizzle melted white chocolate over pastry. Cut into squares or wedges to serve.

Cream Cheese Chocolate Chip Pastry Cookies

Makes 2 dozen

1 (17 1/2 oz.) pkg. frozen
   puff pastry, thawed
1 (8 oz.) pkg. cream cheese,
   softened

3 T. sugar
1 (11 1/2 oz.) pkg. milk
   chocolate chips, divided

Roll out 1 puff pastry sheet into a 10x14" rectangle. In a small bowl, combine cream cheese and sugar, mixing until smooth. Spread half of the cream cheese mixture over puff pastry to within 1" of the edges. Sprinkle half of the milk chocolate chips over cream cheese layer. Starting at long edge of pastry, roll pastry into a log. Seal ends of log by moistening with water. Repeat steps with remaining pastry sheet, cream cheese filling and milk chocolate chips. Chill log in refrigerator for 1 hour. Preheat oven to 375°. Remove logs from refrigerator and cut into 1" thick slices. Place slices on lightly greased baking sheets and bake in oven for 20 to 25 minutes or until golden brown. Let pastries cool on baking sheets for 2 minutes before removing to wire racks.

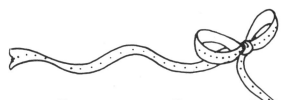

North England Pastry Cakes

Makes 8 servings

2 T. butter
1 C. currants
2 T. chopped candied
    mixed fruit peel
3/4 C. Demerara sugar

3/4 tsp. mixed spice
1/2 (17 1/2 oz.) pkg. frozen
    puff pastry, thawed
1 egg white, beaten
1/4 C. sugar

Preheat oven to 425°. Sprinkle a baking sheet with water. In a small saucepan over medium heat, melt butter. Stir in currants, mixed fruit peel, Demerara sugar and mixed spice. Stir until sugar is dissolved and fruit is evenly coated. Remove from heat. On a lightly floured sugar, roll out 1 puff pastry to 1/4" thickness. Cut out pastry into eight 5" circles. Divide fruit mixture evenly into circles. Moisten edges of pastry circles with water and pull edges up and over filling, pinching to seal. Place cakes on a floured surface and gently roll out filled pastries to make wider circles, being careful not to break the pastry open. Brush each cake with egg white and generously sprinkle with sugar. Make 3 parallel cuts across the top of each pastry cake and place cakes on prepared baking sheet. Bake in oven for 15 minutes or until cakes are golden.

Delicious Baked Dumplings

Makes 8 servings

1 (17 1/2 oz.) pkg. frozen puff pastry, thawed	1 egg, beaten
1 C. sugar	4 Granny Smith apples, peeled, cored and halved
3/8 C. dry bread crumbs	1 C. powdered sugar
3 T. cinnamon	1 tsp. vanilla
Pinch of nutmeg	3 T. milk

Preheat oven to 425°. Lightly grease a baking sheet. Roll out each puff pastry sheet into a 12" square. Cut squares into quarters to make eight 6" squares. In a small bowl, combine sugar, bread crumbs, cinnamon and nutmeg. Brush each pastry square with some beaten egg and place 1 tablespoon bread crumb mixture into the center of each square. Place one apple half, cored side down, over bread crumb mixture. Top with another tablespoon of the bread crumb mixture. Pull up the four corner of one pastry square up and over filling and pinch sides together to seal. Repeat with remaining squares. Brush each dumpling with remaining beaten egg. Place dumplings on a lightly greased baking sheet. Bake in oven for 15 minutes. Reduce oven temperature to 350° and bake for an additional 25 minutes, until lightly browned. Let dumplings cool completely to room temperature. To make icing, in a medium bowl, combine powdered sugar, vanilla and enough milk to make icing desired consistency. Drizzle icing over cooled dumplings. Serve immediately.

No-Bake

Chocolate-Almond Fudge

Makes 4 pounds

4 C. sugar
1 (7 oz.) jar marshmallow
    crème
1 (12 oz.) can evaporated milk
1 T. butter
2 C. chocolate chips

1 (7 oz.) milk chocolate bar,
    broken into pieces
1 tsp. vanilla
3/4 C. chopped almonds,
    toasted*

Line a 9" square pan or 9x13" baking dish with aluminum foil, extending foil over edges of pan. In a large heavy saucepan over medium heat, combine sugar, marshmallow crème, evaporated milk and butter. Cook for 7 minutes, stirring constantly, until mixture comes to a rolling boil. Remove from heat and immediately add chocolate chips and broken milk chocolate bar, stirring until chocolate is melted and mixture is smooth. Stir in vanilla and chopped almonds. Pour mixture into prepared pan. Place pan in refrigerator until firm. Pull up on aluminum foil to lift fudge from pan. Peel off aluminum foil and cut fudge into 1" pieces. Store in an airtight container.

* To toast, place chopped almonds in a single layer on a baking sheet. Bake at 350° for approximately 10 minutes or until almonds are golden brown.

Ladyfinger Cheesecake

Makes 12 servings

2 (11 oz.) pkgs. no-bake
   cheesecake mix
2/3 C. butter or margarine,
   melted
1/4 C. sugar
1 (3 oz.) pkg. ladyfingers
1 (8 oz.) pkg. cream cheese,
   softened

3 C. cold milk, divided
1 (12 oz.) container frozen
   whipped topping, thawed
1 (21 oz.) can raspberry
   pie filling or other
   flavor of choice

In a medium bowl, combine crust mix from cheesecake packages, melted butter and sugar. Mix well and press onto the bottom of an ungreased 10" springform pan. Arrange ladyfingers around edge of pan. In a medium mixing bowl, beat cream cheese and 1/2 cup milk until smooth. Gradually beat in remaining milk. Add filling mix from cheesecake packages and beat until smooth. Beat at medium speed for 3 minutes. Fold in whipped topping and pour filling over crust. Cover and refrigerate at least 1 hour. Top cheesecake with pie filling. Remove sides of pan before serving.

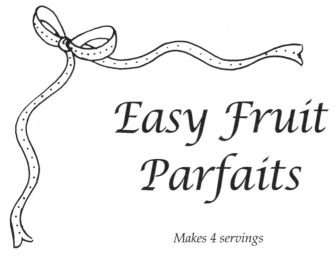

Easy Fruit Parfaits

Makes 4 servings

1 C. boiling water
1 (3 oz.) pkg. red gelatin,
   any flavor
1 C. cold water

1 (15 1/4 oz.) can tropical
   fruit salad, drained
Thawed whipped topping

In a medium bowl, combine boiling water and red gelatin, mixing until completely dissolved. Stir in cold water. Pour gelatin into 4 tall dessert or parfait glasses, filling about half full. Refrigerate filled glasses for 4 hours or until firm. To serve, layer whipped topping over gelatin and place tropical fruit over whipped topping.

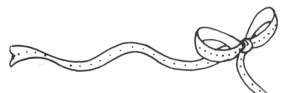

Blender Chocolate Mousse

Makes 8 servings

1 (12 oz.) pkg. chocolate chips   **1 C. hot milk**
1/2 C. sugar   **3 T. brandy**
3 eggs

    In a blender, combine chocolate chips, sugar and eggs. Blend until smooth and add hot milk and brandy. Blend again and pour mixture into 8 small serving cups and refrigerate at least 1 hour.

Warning
Eating raw eggs is not recommended for pregnant women, the elderly and the sick because there is a risk that eggs may be contaminated with salmonella bacteria.

Strawberry Freeze

Makes 18 servings

3/4 C. sugar
1 (8 oz.) pkg. cream cheese,
    softened
1 (20 oz.) can crushed
    pineapple, drained

1 (10 oz.) pkg. frozen sliced
    strawberries, thawed
2 bananas, diced
1 (8 oz.) container frozen
    whipped topping, thawed

In a medium bowl, cream together sugar and cream cheese until smooth. In a separate bowl, combine crushed pineapple, thawed strawberries, diced bananas and whipped topping. Fold fruit mixture into cream cheese mixture and mix until evenly blended. Spread mixture into a 9x13" baking dish. Cover with plastic wrap and freeze for 8 hours or overnight. Remove from freezer 20 minutes before serving.

Angel Pudding

Makes 10 servings

1 (10") angel food cake
1 (6 oz.) pkg. instant
    chocolate pudding mix
1 (5 oz.) pkg. instant
    vanilla pudding mix

6 C. cold milk
2 (2.1 oz.) Butterfinger
    candy bars, crushed

Cut angel food cake into 1" cubes. In the bottom of a 9x13" baking dish, place half of the angel food cake cubes. In two separate bowls, prepared chocolate and vanilla puddings with cold milk according to package directions. Spread prepared chocolate pudding over cake is baking dish. Top with half of the crushed Butterfingers. Spread remaining angel food cake cubes over crushed candy bars and spread prepared vanilla pudding over angel food cake. Chill in refrigerator until ready to serve.

Honey Nut Cookies

Makes 4 dozen

16 graham crackers
1 C. crunchy peanut butter
2/3 C. honey

1/2 C. evaporated milk
1 C. shredded coconut

Crush the graham crackers in a food processor or between 2 pieces of wax paper using a rolling pin. In a large mixing bowl, combine peanut butter, honey and evaporated milk. Mix well. Stir in crushed graham crackers. Make small balls with dough and place on waxed paper. Roll balls in shredded coconut.

Peanut Butter Dreams

Makes 4 to 5 dozen

1/2 C. butter	**3 C. crispy rice cereal**
4 C. powdered sugar	**2 C. chocolate chips**
2 C. creamy peanut butter	**4 T. shortening**

In a large mixing bowl, combine butter, powdered sugar, peanut butter and crispy rice cereal. Mix well. Roll mixture into small balls and set aside. In a small saucepan over low heat, melt chocolate chips and shortening. Remove from heat. Coat the balls in the chocolate mixture. Refrigerate for several hours.

Fruit & Nut Clusters

Makes 3 to 4 dozen

**1 (12 oz.) pkg. white
   baking chips
2 C. sweetened rice and
   corn cereal squares**

**1 C. dried fruit, such as
   cranberries, raisins,
   diced apricots
1/4 C. peanuts**

In a large microwave-safe bowl, heat white chocolate chips in microwave, stopping to stir every 30 seconds, until completely melted. Gently stir in cereal squares, fruit and peanuts. Mix until well coated. Drop by tablespoonfuls onto waxed paper. Refrigerate for 1 hour. Cover and store in a cool place.

Jimmy Carter Drop Cookies

Makes 4 to 5 dozen

2/3 C. sugar
2/3 C. white corn syrup
1 tsp. vanilla

1 1/4 C. chunky peanut butter
3 C. corn flakes

In a large saucepan over heat, combine sugar and corn syrup. Bring to a boil and add vanilla and peanut butter. Stir until well mixed. Gently mix in corn flakes. Drop by tablespoonfuls onto waxed paper.

Chocolate Peanut Butter Pie

Makes 8 servings

4 oz. cream cheese, softened
1 T. sugar
2 C. plus 1 T. milk, divided
1 C. peanut butter
1 (8 oz.) container frozen
    whipped topping,
    thawed, divided

1 (9") prepared graham
    cracker crust
2 (3.9 oz.) pkgs. instant
    chocolate pudding mix
4 peanut butter cups,
    cut into 1/2" pieces

In a large bowl, combine cream cheese, sugar, 1 tablespoon milk and peanut butter until smooth. Gently stir in 1 1/2 cups whipped topping. Spread mixture evenly over the bottom of the prepared pie crust. In a separate bowl, combine chocolate pudding mix with remaining 2 cups milk. Mix well until thick. Immediately fold in remaining whipped topping. Spread mixture evenly over layer in pie crust. Scatter peanut butter cup pieces over top of pie. Cover and refrigerate for 4 hours before serving. Store in refrigerator.

Quick and Easy Lemon Pie

Makes 8 servings

1 (4.3 oz.) pkg. non-instant lemon pudding mix
1 (8 oz.) pkg. cream cheese, softened
1/2 (14 oz.) can sweetened condensed milk
3 T. lemon juice
1 (9") prepared graham cracker crust
1 (8 oz) container frozen whipped topping, thawed

In a large saucepan, prepare lemon pudding according to package directions. When pudding thickens, reduce heat to low. Stir in softened cream cheese, sweetened condensed milk and lemon juice, making sure to stir frequently as mixture may stick to saucepan. Pour mixture into prepared pie crust. Cover and chill in refrigerator. Before serving, spread whipped topping evenly over pie. Store in refrigerator.

Freezer Chocolate Mint Pie

Makes 8 servings

2 1/2 C. crushed Oreo
    cookies, divided
1/4 C. butter, melted
1 qt. mint chocolate chip
    ice cream, softened,
    divided

4 T. plus 2 tsp. crème
    de menthe liqueur, divided
3 egg whites
Salt to taste
1/4 tsp. cream of tartar
1/3 C. sugar

In a large bowl, combine 1 1/2 cups crushed Oreo cookies and melted butter. Press mixture firmly onto bottom and up sides of a 9" pie pan. Freeze for 1 to 2 hours. Spread half of softened mint chocolate chip ice cream into prepared crust. Drizzle 2 tablespoons crème de menthe liqueur evenly over ice cream and sprinkle 1/2 cup crushed Oreo cookies over ice cream. Repeat layers with remaining ice cream, 2 tablespoons crème de menthe and remaining 1/2 cup crushed Oreo cookies. In a medium mixing bowl, beat egg whites until foamy. Add salt and cream of tartar and beat until mixture is slightly stiff. Gradually beat in sugar until soft peaks form. Fold in remaining 2 teaspoons crème de menthe liqueur. Spread mixture evenly over pie. Freeze up to 24 hours. Just before serving, place pie in broiler until top is golden. Store in freezer.

The Best Blueberry Pie

Makes 8 servings

**4 C. fresh blueberries,
    divided
1 (8") pie crust, baked
    and cooled
1 T. flour**

**1 T. butter
1 T. lemon juice
1/2 C. sugar
Whipped topping, optional**

Pour 2 cups blueberries into prepared and cooled pie crust. In a medium saucepan, combine flour, butter, lemon juice and sugar. Mix well. Add remaining 2 cups blueberries. Bring mixture just to a boil over medium heat, until berries begin to pop open. Pour cooked berries over fresh berries in pie crust. Chill pie in refrigerator until ready to serve. If desired, serve with whipped topping. Store at room temperature or in refrigerator.

Simple Salted Nut Rolls

Makes 2 dozen

1 can sweetened condensed milk	3 C. miniature marshmallows
1 (12 oz.) pkg. peanut butter chips	3 (12 oz.) jars salted or dry roasted peanuts, divided

In a microwave-safe bowl, combine sweetened condensed milk, peanut butter chips and marshmallows. Microwave for about 2 1/2 minutes, until melted. Spread 1 jar of peanuts into a greased 9x13" pan. Spread marshmallow mixture over peanuts. Top with remaining 2 jars of peanuts and press down lightly. Refrigerate and cut into bars.

Chocolate Puffed Wheat Bars

Makes 16 servings

8 C. puffed wheat cereal
3 T. cocoa powder
1/3 C. corn syrup

1/4 C. brown sugar
1/3 C. butter or margarine

Grease a 9x9" pan and set aside. In a large bowl, place puffed wheat cereal and set aside. Grease the rim of a medium saucepan to prevent boil over. In saucepan, combine cocoa powder, corn syrup, brown sugar and butter. Cook over medium heat, stirring often, until mixture comes to a full boil. Allow to boil for 1 minute before removing from heat. Pour chocolate mixture over cereal and stir until evenly coated. Using a greased spatula, press mixture into the prepared pan. Allow to cool before cutting into squares. Wrap squares individually or store in an air-tight container.

Cheerio and M&M Bars

Makes 1 1/2 dozen

4 T. margarine
1 (10 1/2 oz.) pkg. miniature marshmallows

1/2 C. peanut butter
5 C. Cheerios
1 C. M&M's

Grease a 9x13" baking dish and set aside. In a large microwave-safe bowl, microwave margarine for 45 seconds or until melted. Add marshmallows and stir to coat. Return to the microwave for an additional 1 1/2 minutes, stirring after 45 seconds. Mix in peanut butter and immediately stir in toasted oat cereal. Add M&M's and mix well. Transfer mixture to prepared pan and press down with a greased spatula until evenly spread. Allow to cool before cutting into squares.

Chewy Chocolate Peanut Bars

Makes 4 dozen

1 C. corn syrup
3/4 C. peanut butter
1 1/2 C. chocolate chips

1 tsp. vanilla
2 1/2 C. quick cooking oats
1 3/4 C. unsalted peanuts

In a medium saucepan over medium heat, combine corn syrup, peanut butter and chocolate chips. Bring to a boil, stirring constantly. Continue to boil for 5 minutes. Remove from heat and stir in vanilla, oats and peanuts. Turn onto a greased 10x15" jellyroll pan. Let mixture slightly cool before pressing down into pan. Refrigerate overnight. Let stand for 20 minutes before cutting into squares.

Crispy Caramel Treats

Makes 32 servings

4 (2.05 oz.) Milky Way bars
3/4 C. butter or margarine,
divided

3 C. crispy rice cereal
1 C. milk chocolate chips

In microwave or a double boiler, melt candy bars and 1/2 cup butter, stirring occasionally, until smooth. Stir in cereal until well coated. Press mixture into a greased 7x11" pan. In a separate microwave-safe bowl or double boiler, melt chocolate chips and remaining 1/4 cup butter, stirring until smooth. Remove from heat and spread chocolate mixture over ingredients in pan. Refrigerate 1 hour, or until firm, before cutting into squares.

Fancy Schmancy

Tiramisu Torte

Makes 16 servings

4 eggs, separated
1 1/4 C. sugar, divided
1/2 C. plus 3 T. water, divided
1 tsp. vanilla, divided
3/4 C. flour
1 tsp. baking powder
2 T. instant espresso powder

2 T. dark rum
1/2 C. powdered sugar
2 (8 oz.) pkgs. mascarpone
   or cream cheese
3 (1 oz.) squares semi-sweet
   baking chocolate, grated
2 C. whipped topping

Preheat oven to 375°. Lightly grease a 10x15" jelly roll pan and line pan with waxed paper. Grease the waxed paper and set aside. In a large mixing bowl, beat egg whites at high speed until foamy. Continue beating and gradually add 1/4 cup sugar, until stiff peaks form. In a small mixing bowl, combine 1/2 cup sugar, egg yolks, 3 tablespoons water and 1/2 teaspoon vanilla. Beat at high speed about 5 to 6 minutes, scraping bowl often. Gently stir in flour and baking powder by hand. Gently stir in egg yolk mixture and beaten egg whites. Pour batter into prepared pan. Bake in oven for 14 to 18 minutes or until cake springs back when gently pressed. Let cool completely on a wire rack. In a 1 quart saucepan over medium heat, combine remaining 1/2 cup sugar, remaining 1/2 cup water and espresso powder. Bring to a boil for 1 minute and stir in rum. Let cool completely. Cut cake crosswise into 3 rounds. Brush each cake generously with rum mixture, reserving 2 tablespoons rum mixture. In a medium bowl, combine powdered sugar, mascarpone cheese and remaining 1/2 teaspoon vanilla. Stir in 2/3 of the grated chocolate. Place 1 cake on serving plate and spread half of the powdered sugar mixture over cake. Top with another cake and spread remaining half of frosting over cake. Top with the third cake. In a chilled large bowl, combine whipped topping and reserved rum mixture. Spread mixture over top and sides of cake. Sprinkle remaining grated chocolate over cake.

Napoleons

Makes 20 servings

1 1/2 (17 1/2 oz.) pkgs. frozen
    puff pastry, thawed
1/4 C. cornstarch
4 C. milk, divided
1/3 C. cake flour
7/8 C. sugar, divided
3 eggs, separated

1 T. butter
1 tsp. vanilla
1 (12 oz.) jar apricot jam
3 C. powdered sugar, sifted
1 T. lemon juice
Drops of red food coloring

Preheat oven to 350°. Roll out 3 puff pastry sheets to same size rectangles, about 1/8" thick. Prick pastry with a fork and place on ungreased baking sheets. Bake in oven for about 10 minutes, until pastry is golden. In a medium bowl, combine cornstarch and 1/2 cup milk, mixing with fingers until smooth. Stir in cake flour and half of the sugar. Beat in egg yolks and set aside. In a medium saucepan over medium heat, bring remaining 3 1/2 cups milk and remaining half of the sugar to a rolling boil. Stir in cornstarch mixture and return to a boil. Remove from heat and stir in butter and vanilla. Let cool completely. In a small saucepan over medium heat or in microwave, heat apricot jam until melted and runny. Place 1 sheet pastry on a cutting board. Spread cooled pastry cream over pastry to 1/2" thickness. Place a second pastry sheet over cream mixture. Brush melted apricot jam over pastry. Top with final pastry sheet and gently press down to compress layers. To make icing, in a medium bowl, combine powdered sugar and lemon juice. Add enough egg whites to make icing a creamy consistency. Transfer a small portion of the icing to a separate bowl and color with red food coloring. Spread remaining icing over top and sides of pastry. Pipe parallel lines of red icing over top of dessert and run a toothpick through lines for a fancy design. Let icing set before cutting into bars.

Marjolaine (Chocolate Lasagna)

Makes 10 servings

1/2 (17 1/2 oz.) pkg. frozen puff pastry, thawed	4 oz. light cream cheese, softened
1/4 C. finely chopped hazelnuts	1/2 C. brown sugar
1 C. chopped semi-sweet chocolate	3 T. strong brewed coffee, cold
2 C. heavy cream	1/2 C. ground hazelnuts
	1/2 C. ground almonds

Preheat oven to 450°. Line a baking sheet with parchment paper. On a lightly floured surface, roll puff pastry sheet into a 13" square. Trim pastry to a 12" square and cut into 3 equal strips, each 4"x12". Poke each strip with a folk and arrange on prepared baking sheet. Sprinkle chopped hazelnuts over each pastry strip. Bake in oven for 8 to 10 minutes, until puffed and golden brown. Let cool completely. If pastries are not the same size, trim pastry with a serrated knife. In a double boiler, melt chopped chocolate, mixing until smooth. Let cool to room temperature. In a large bowl, beat together cream cheese, brown sugar and coffee until smooth. Blend in melted chocolate. Fold in ground hazelnuts and ground almonds. In a large mixing bowl, beat heavy cream until soft peaks form. Fold 1/3 of the whipped cream into the cream cheese mixture and quickly fold in remaining whipped cream. Spread 1/3 of the filling over each strip of puff pastry. Stack layers of pastry. Chill in refrigerator for 3 hours or until pastry is set. Using a serrated knife, gently cut pastry into 10 slices.

Raspberry Cream Jelly Roll

Makes 15 servings

1/3 C. cake flour, sifted
2 T. cornstarch
4 large eggs, separated
1/2 C. plus 1 T. sugar
2 tsp. vanilla
2 T. butter, melted

1/4 tsp. cream of tartar
1 C. heavy cream
1 C. seedless raspberry jam, divided
1/4 C. powdered sugar

Preheat oven to 400°. Line a jelly roll pan with aluminum foil and lightly grease and flour the foil. In a medium bowl, whisk together cake flour and cornstarch. In a medium mixing bowl, beat egg yolks at medium high speed. Slowly add 1/2 cup sugar and beat for about 5 minutes, until lightened and fluffy. Add vanilla and melted butter and beat at low speed until smooth. Fold in flour mixture in batches until thoroughly incorporated. In a separate mixing bowl, beat egg whites at high speed until frothy. Add cream of tartar and beat until soft peaks form. Add remaining 1 tablespoon sugar and beat until stiff peaks form. Add 1/3 of the egg whites mixture to the batter, mixing gently. Add remaining egg whites mixture and stir gently until well incorporated. Pour batter into prepared pan and bake in oven for 8 to 12 minutes, until top of cake springs back when gently pressed. Transfer pan to a wire rack, cover with a damp towel and let cool for 5 minutes. Remove towel and transfer cake to a flat surface, foiled side down. In a medium mixing bowl, beat heavy cream at high speed until thickened. Fold in 1/2 cup raspberry jam. Melt remaining 1/2 cup jam in microwave or in a double boiler, stirring until smooth. Spread melted jam over cooled cake. Spread filling over cake to within 1" of the edges. Starting at a long side, gently and slowly roll up cake, removing foil as cake is rolled. Transfer cake, seam side down, to a serving platter. Dust top of roll with powdered sugar. Cut roll into 1" slices before serving.

Chocolate Mint Layered Torte

Makes 16 servings

2 C. flour
1 1/2 C. plus 2 T. sugar,
  divided
1/2 C. cocoa powder
1/2 C. plus 2 T. butter,
  softened, divided
1 C. water
3 eggs

1 1/4 tsp. baking powder
1 tsp. baking soda
1 tsp. vanilla
2 C. heavy cream
1 3/4 tsp. mint extract, divided
1/2 C. chocolate chips
2 T. light corn syrup

Preheat oven to 350°. Grease two 9" round cake pans and set aside. Line each pan with waxed paper and grease the waxed paper. In a large mixing bowl, combine flour, 1 1/2 cups sugar, cocoa powder, 1/2 cup butter, water, eggs, baking powder, baking soda and vanilla, beating at medium speed until smooth. Pour batter into prepared pans. Bake in oven for 20 to 25 minutes or until a toothpick inserted in center of cakes comes out clean. Let cool for 10 minutes before removing from pans. Remove waxed paper. In a small mixing bowl, beat heavy cream and 1 1/2 teaspoons mint extract at high speed, until soft peaks form. Continue beating for 1 to 2 minutes and gradually add remaining 2 tablespoons sugar. Using a serrated knife, cut each cake layer in half horizontally. To assemble torte, place 1 cake layer half on a serving plate. Set aside 1/2 cup of the filling. Spread 1/3 of the remaining filling over cake layer. Repeat with remaining cake layers and filling. Chill torte in refrigerator for 1 hour. In a medium saucepan, melt remaining 2 tablespoons butter. Add chocolate chips and corn syrup, stirring constantly, until melted. Remove from heat and stir in remaining 1/4 teaspoon mint extract. Spread glaze over top of torte. Garnish with reserved 1/2 cup filling. Chill in refrigerator until ready to serve.

Glazed Apricot, Almond & Chocolate Torte

Makes 8 servings

3/4 C. diced dried and
   glazed apricots
1 tsp. cocoa powder
1 C. flour
1/3 C. cake flour
1/4 tsp. baking powder
1/2 tsp. salt
1 C. butter, melted
4 (1 oz.) squares unsweetened
   baking chocolate, melted

3 oz. bittersweet chocolate,
   melted
4 large eggs
1 3/4 C. sugar
1 3/4 C. sugar
2 tsp. vanilla
3/4 tsp. almond extract, divided
1/3 C. slivered almonds
3/4 C. plus 2 T. apricot
   preserves

Preheat oven to 325°. Grease the bottom and sides of a 9"
springform pan. Lay diced apricots of a sheet of waxed paper. Sprinkle
cocoa powder over apricots until lightly coated and set aside. Into a
medium bowl, sift flour, cake flour, baking powder and salt. In a
separate bowl, combine melted butter, melted unsweetened chocolate
and melted bittersweet chocolate, mixing until well combined. In a
large mixing bowl, beat eggs at low speed. Add sugar and continue
beat for 1 minute. Blend in melted chocolate mixture. Add vanilla and
1/2 teaspoon almond extract. Add sifted flour mixture and mix well.
Batter should be moderately thick. Stir in apricot pieces and slivered
almonds. Pour batter into prepared pan. Bake in oven for 45 to 50
minutes, until set. Let cake cool on a wire rack. When completely
cooled, remove sides of pan. In a small saucepan over medium high
heat, bring apricot preserves to a rapid simmer, stirring occasionally.
Strain preserves in a fined sieve and stir in remaining 1/4 teaspoon
almond extract. Immediately spread glaze over torte. Let glaze set
before cutting torte into slices.

91

Tuxedo Strawberries

Makes 1 1/2 dozen

18 medium fresh strawberries
   with stems
1 C. white chocolate chips

3 1/2 tsp. shortening, divided
1 1/3 C. chocolate chips

Line a tray or baking sheet with waxed paper and set aside. Wash strawberries and pat until completely dry. In a double boiler, melt white chocolate chips and 1 1/2 teaspoon shortening, mixing until smooth. Dip each strawberry into the melted white chocolate almost up to the stems, forming the "shirt". Place on prepared tray and chill in refrigerator for 30 minutes, until set. In a double boiler, melt chocolate chips and remaining 2 teaspoons shortening, mixing until smooth. To makes the "jacket", dip each side of the strawberry, leaving a "V" of white chocolate showing in the center. Set aside remaining chocolate. Chill strawberries in refrigerator for an additional 30 minutes, until set. If necessary, re-melt remaining chocolate and transfer to a pastry bag or heavy duty resealable plastic bag, cutting a small hole in the bottom corner. If using a pastry bag, insert a #2 pastry tip. Pipe a chocolate "bow tie" at the top of the white chocolate shirt. Pipe three buttons down the front of each shirt. Chill in refrigerator for 30 minutes or until set. Completed strawberries can be stored in an airtight container in refrigerator for 1 day.

English Trifle

Makes 14 servings

2 pints fresh strawberries
1/4 C. sugar
2 bananas, sliced
1/4 C. orange juice
1 (4 serving size) pkg. instant vanilla pudding mix
2 C. milk
2 (8" or 9") white cake layers, baked and cooled
1 pint fresh blueberries
1 C. heavy cream
1/4 C. blanched slivered almonds
12 maraschino cherries

Slice strawberries and sprinkle with sugar. Place sliced bananas in a medium bowl and toss with orange juice. In a medium bowl, prepare vanilla pudding mix according to package directions, using 2 cups milk. Cut the cake layers into 1" cubes. In a large glass bowl, cover the bottom with half of the cake cubes. Layer half of the strawberries over cake, followed by half of the blueberries then half of the bananas. Spread half of the pudding over the bananas and repeat layers with remaining cake cubes, strawberries, blueberries, bananas and pudding. In a medium mixing bowl, beat heavy cream at medium high speed until stiff peaks form. Spread whipped cream over pudding layer. Garnish with slivered almonds and cherries.

Lemon Macaroon Tartlets

Makes 2 dozen

3 C. shredded coconut, divided
1/2 C. sugar
3/8 C. flour
1 tsp. vanilla
2 egg whites
1 (4 serving size) pkg. instant lemon pudding mix
1 (8 oz.) container frozen whipped topping, thawed

Preheat oven to 400°. Lightly grease 24 mini muffin cups. In a medium bowl, combine 2 cups shredded coconut, sugar, flour, vanilla and egg whites, mixing well. Divide mixture evenly into prepared muffing cups, pressing mixture up sides and onto bottoms of cups. Bake in oven until edges are browned. Let cool on a wire rack. Prepare lemon pudding mix according to package directions. Spoon lemon pudding evenly into each tartlet shell. Top each tartlet with 2 tablespoons whipped topping and sprinkle tops of tartlets with remaining 1 cup shredded coconut.

Cream Puffs

Makes 20 servings

2 (4 serving size each) pkgs. instant vanilla pudding mix	1/2 C. butter
	1 C. water
	1/4 tsp. salt
2 C. heavy cream	1 C. flour
1 C. milk	4 eggs

In a medium bowl, combine vanilla pudding mix, heavy cream and milk, mixing until smooth. Chill in refrigerator until set. Preheat oven to 425°. In a large pot, bring butter and water to a rolling boil. Stir in salt and flour until mixture forms a ball. Transfer dough to a large mixing bowl and add eggs, one at a time, beating well after each addition. Drop dough by tablespoonfuls onto a lightly greased baking sheet. Bake in oven for 20 to 25 minutes or until golden brown. When shells are cooled, either split open pastries and fill with pudding mixture or use a pastry bag to pipe pudding into shells.

Apple Crumble Tart

Makes 8 servings

3/8 C. flour
3/8 C. chopped blanched
   almonds
1/2 C. plus 3 T. sugar, divided
1/4 tsp. cinnamon
3 T. butter, chilled
1/4 tsp. vanilla

1/2 (17 1/2 oz.) pkg. frozen
   puff pastry, thawed
1 T. butter, melted
3 apples, peeled, cored
   and chopped
3 egg yolks
1/3 C. dry Marsala wine

Preheat oven to 350°. In a small bowl, combine flour, almonds, 1/2 cup sugar and cinnamon. Using a pastry blender, mix in 3 tablespoons chilled butter and vanilla, mixing until small crumbs form. Unfold 1 puff pastry sheet and cut into a 10" circle. Place circle pastry on a baking sheet and brush 1 tablespoon melted butter over pastry. Arrange chopped apples in the center of the pastry, spreading to within 1/2" of the edge. Spoon crumb mixture over apples, being careful not to spill over edges of pastry. Bake in oven for 30 minutes, or until golden brown. In a double boiler, combine egg yolks and remaining 3 tablespoons sugar. Using an electric mixer, beat mixture constantly. When mixture is foamy, add Marsala wine and continue beating until mixture thickens, being careful not to overcook. Remove from heat. To serve, cut apple crumble mixture into slices and place in serving bowls. Spoon warm wine mixture over apple crumble in each serving bowl.

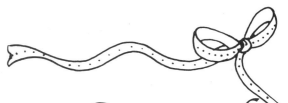

Fancy Caramel Brownies

Makes 3 dozen

**1 (18 1/4 oz.) pkg. chocolate
   cake mix
1/2 C. butter, melted
1/3 C. milk**

**2 eggs
1 C. chocolate chips
1 C. toffee baking bits
35 Rolo candies, unwrapped**

Preheat oven to 350°. Grease a 9x13" baking dish and set aside. In a large bowl, combine chocolate cake mix, melted butter, milk and eggs, stirring until well blended. Press half of the mixture into the bottom of the prepared pan and bake in oven for 6 minutes. Remove from oven and sprinkle chocolate chips and toffee baking bits over crust. Lightly press Rolo candies over chocolate chips and toffee bits. Crumble remaining cake mixture over Rolo candies. Return to oven for an additional 20 to 25 minutes, or until a toothpick inserted in center of brownies comes out clean. Let cool on a wire rack before cutting into squares.

Divinity

Makes 18 servings

2 C. sugar	1/4 tsp. salt
1/2 C. light corn syrup	2 egg whites
1/2 C. hot water	1 tsp. vanilla

In a large saucepan over medium heat, combine sugar, corn syrup, hot water and salt. Cook, stirring frequently, until sugar dissolves and mixture comes to a boil. Let mixture cook to hard ball stage (250°) without stirring. Using a pastry brush dipped in water, frequently wipe down crystals forming on sides of pan. Remove from heat. Just as syrup mixture is reaching temperature, in a large glass mixing bowl, beat egg whites until stiff peaks form. Pour hot syrup mixture in a thin stream over egg whites mixture, beating at medium speed. Increase speed to high and continue beating for 5 minutes. Add vanilla and continue beating until mixture becomes stiff and begins to lose its glossiness. If mixture becomes too stiff, add a few drops of hot water. Immediately drop mixture by teaspoonfuls onto waxed paper. For a decorative flair, twirl tops of divinity with the spoon when dropping. Let stand until set. Store divinity at room temperature in an airtight container.

Baked Alaska

Makes 16 servings

2 qts. vanilla ice cream, softened	1/2 tsp. almond extract
1 (18 1/4 oz.) pkg. white cake mix	8 egg whites
	1/8 tsp. cream of tartar
1 egg	1/8 tsp. salt
	1 C. sugar

Line the bottom and sides of an 8" round bowl with aluminum foil. Spread vanilla ice cream over aluminum foil, packing down firmly. Cover and place bowl in freezer for 8 hours, or until firm. Preheat oven to 350°. Grease and flour an 8" square pan. In a medium bowl, prepare cake mix according to package directions, using 1 egg and 1/2 teaspoon almond extract. Pour mixture into prepared square pan. Bake according to package directions, until a toothpick inserted in center of cake comes out clean. In a medium mixing bowl, beat egg whites, cream of tartar, salt and sugar until stiff peaks form. Line a baking sheet with parchment paper. Place baked and cooled cake in center of baking sheet. Turn molded ice cream out onto cake and remove aluminum foil. Quickly spread egg whites mixture evenly over ice cream and cake, all the way down to the parchment paper. Return to freezer for 2 hours. Preheat oven to 425°. Bake cake in oven on lowest rack for 8 to 10 minutes or until lightly browned. Serve immediately.

Run for the Roses Pie

Makes 6 to 8 servings

3/4 C. chocolate chips	1/2 C. flour
1 C. chopped walnuts	2 eggs, slightly beaten
1 (8") unbaked pie crust	1 T. bourbon
1/2 C. butter, melted	1 C. whipped topping
3/4 C. sugar	8 maraschino cherries

Preheat oven to 350°. Spread chocolate chips and chopped walnuts evenly over bottom of prepared pie crust. In a large mixing bowl, combine melted butter and sugar. Add flour and mix until smooth. Add beaten eggs and bourbon to the butter mixture. Pour mixture over chocolate chips and walnuts in pie crust. Bake in oven for 30 to 40 minutes. Remove from oven and let cool slightly on a wire rack. If desired, garnish top of pie with whipped topping and cherries.

Diabetic

Tiramisu Parfait

Makes 6 servings

3 1/2 tsp. instant decaffeinated coffee
1 1/2 C. hot water
1 prepared sugar-free angel food cake
1/2 C. mascarpone cheese

1 (8 oz.) pkg. fat-free cream cheese, softened
2 T. dark brown sugar
1 C. granulated artificial sweetener
1/2 tsp. vanilla
2 tsp. cocoa powder, divided

In a small bowl, dissolve instant coffee in hot water and chill mixture in refrigerator. Cut angel food cake into 1" cubes and set aside. In a medium mixing bowl, beat together mascarpone cheese and cream cheese until smooth. Add 2 tablespoons chilled coffee mixture, brown sugar, artificial sweetener and vanilla. Mix well and set aside. Pour remaining cold coffee into a large shallow dish. Quickly dip half of the angel food pieces into the coffee and then place cake pieces in a medium glass serving bowl. Spread half of the cheese mixture over cake. Sprinkle 1 teaspoon cocoa powder over cheese mixture. Repeat layers with remaining angel food cake, cheese mixture and cocoa powder. Cover and chill in refrigerator for 3 hours or overnight.

Fruit Baked Apples

Makes 8 servings

1/2 C. granulated artificial sweetener	2 C. apple cider or apple juice
1 T. cornstarch	1 (6 oz.) pkg. dried mixed fruit, chopped
Pinch of cinnamon	1 T. butter or margarine
Pinch of nutmeg	8 tart baking apples

Preheat oven to 350°. In a medium saucepan over medium heat, combine artificial sweetener, cornstarch, cinnamon and nutmeg. Stir in apple cider and add chopped dried fruit. Heat until mixture boils, reduce heat and let simmer for 10 to 15 minutes or until fruit is tender and mixture is reduced to about 1 cup. Add butter and stir until melted. Remove cores from tart apples, making sure not to cut through to the bottom. Remove 1" peel from the top of each apple and place apples in a greased baking dish. Fill the center of each apple with fruit from mixture and spoon juices from mixture over apples. Bake in oven, uncovered, for about 45 minutes or until apples are tender.

Cinnamon Raisin Bread Pudding

Makes 6 servings

2 C. skim milk
2/3 C. granulated artificial
    sweetener
4 T. butter or margarine,
    melted
1 egg

2 egg whites
1 tsp. cinnamon
1/4 tsp. salt
4 C. day-old cinnamon raisin
    bread, cut into 3/4" cubes

Preheat oven to 350°. In a large bowl, combine milk, artificial sweetener, melted butter, egg, egg whites, cinnamon and salt. Stir in bread cubes. Spoon mixture into an ungreased 1 1/2 quart baking dish. Bake in oven for 30 to 35 minutes or until pudding is set and a toothpick inserted in center of pudding comes out clean.

Chocolate Chip Fudgie Cups

Makes 2 dozen

6 T. plus 1/3 C. butter or margarine, softened, divided	1 3/4 C. flour, divided
	1/2 tsp. baking soda
	1/2 tsp. salt, divided
3 eggs, divided	1/2 C. mini chocolate chips
2 tsp. vanilla, divided	6 T. cocoa powder
1 1/3 C. granulated artificial sweetener, divided	1/3 C. chopped nuts
	1 tsp. baking powder
1/3 C. brown sugar	1/2 C. unsweetened applesauce

In a medium mixing bowl, beat 1/3 cup butter until fluffy. Add 1 egg and 1 teaspoon vanilla and beat until well blended. Mix in 1/3 cup artificial sweetener and brown sugar. In a separate bowl, combine 1 cup flour, baking soda and 1/4 teaspoon salt. Add flour mixture to butter mixture and stir in mini chocolate chips. Mix well and pat dough into 1/2" thick circle. Wrap dough tightly in plastic wrap and place in freezer while preparing filling. Preheat oven to 350°. To make filling, in a medium bowl, combine remaining 1 cup artificial sweetener, remaining 3/4 cup flour, cocoa powder, chopped nuts, baking powder and remaining 1/4 teaspoon salt. In a medium mixing bowl, beat together applesauce, remaining 6 tablespoons butter, remaining 2 eggs and remaining 1 teaspoon vanilla. Stir flour mixture into applesauce mixture and blend well. Lightly grease 24 mini muffin cups. Remove dough from freezer and press about 1 tablespoon dough into the bottom and up sides of each cup. Fill each cup with filling. Bake in oven for 15 to 18 minutes.

Special Oatmeal Cookies

Makes 3 dozen

1 1/2 C. rolled oats	1/2 tsp. salt
2/3 C. butter, melted	2 tsp. baking powder
4 egg whites	1/2 C. milk
1 C. granulated artificial sweetener	1 tsp. vanilla
	1/2 C. raisins
1 1/2 C. flour	1/2 C. chopped walnuts

Preheat oven to 375°. Lightly grease baking sheets and set aside. In a medium bowl, combine oats and melted butter. Add egg whites and artificial sweetener, blending until smooth. In a separate bowl, combine flour, salt and baking powder. Alternating, add flour mixture, milk and vanilla to oats mixture, stirring well after each addition. Stir in raisins and chopped walnuts. Drop dough by teaspoonfuls, 1" to 2" apart, on prepared baking sheets. Bake in oven for 10 to 15 minutes.

Raspberry-Almond Bar Cookies

Makes 2 dozen

2 C. flour
1/2 C. granulated artificial
   sweetener
1/8 tsp. salt
1/2 C. cold butter or margarine,
   cut into pieces

1 egg
1 T. water
1 tsp. grated lemon peel
1 (10 oz.) jar seedless raspberry
   preserves
1/4 C. sliced almonds, toasted*

Preheat oven to 375°. In a medium bowl, combine flour, artificial sweetener and salt. Using a pastry blender, cut in pieces of butter until mixture is crumbly. Mix in egg, water and grated lemon peel. Press mixture into the bottom of a well greased 7x11" baking dish. Bake in oven for 12 to 15 minutes or until edges of crust are lightly browned. Remove from oven and spread raspberry preserves over crust. Sprinkle toasted almonds over raspberry preserves. Return to oven and bake for an additional 12 to 15 minutes or until raspberry filling is bubbly. Let cool completely on a wire rack before cutting into bars.

Thumbprint Cookies

Makes 2 dozen

6 T. butter or margarine	1 1/4 C. flour
1 C. granulated artificial sweetener	1/4 tsp. baking powder
	1/4 tsp. baking soda
1 egg	1/4 tsp. salt
2 T. milk	3/4 C. sugar-free preserves
1 tsp. vanilla	or spreadable fruit of choice

Preheat oven to 350°. Lightly grease baking sheets and set aside. In a medium mixing bowl, beat together butter and artificial sweetener until well combined. Mix in egg, milk and vanilla and blend well. Gradually beat in flour, baking powder, baking soda and salt. Mix well and shape teaspoonfuls of dough into balls. Place dough on prepared baking sheets. Press thumb deeply into dough to form a thumbprint indentation. Bake in oven for 11 to 13 minutes. Remove from oven and cool cookies completely on wire racks. Fill each cooled cookie with about 1/2 teaspoon preserves or spreadable fruit before serving.

Peanut Butter Nuggets

Makes 30 bars

1/2 C. natural peanut butter
1/4 C. dry milk powder
1/4 C. unsweetened shredded
   coconut
1/3 C. rolled oats

1/2 tsp. cinnamon
1/4 C. wheat germ
1/4 C. unsweetened apple juice
   concentrate, thawed

In a large bowl, combine peanut butter, milk powder and shredded coconut. Mix thoroughly and stir in rolled oats, cinnamon, wheat germ and apple juice concentrate. Shape dough into 1" balls and chill in refrigerator for 1 hour before serving. Store leftovers in refrigerator.

Tangy Lemon Squares

Makes 16 servings

3/4 C. flour	1 T. plus 1 tsp. grated lemon
3/4 C. plus 1/3 C. granulated	peel, divided
artificial sweetener, divided	1 tsp. vanilla
1/8 tsp. salt	2 eggs
10 T. butter or margarine,	1/2 C. lemon juice
divided	

Preheat oven to 350°. In a medium bowl, combine flour, 1/3 cup artificial sweetener and salt. Using a pastry blender, cut in 6 tablespoons butter until mixture is crumbly. Add 1 teaspoon grated lemon peel and vanilla. Mix well by hand to form a dough. Press dough evenly onto the bottom and 1/4" up sides of an 8" square baking pan. Bake in oven for 8 to 10 minutes. To make filling, in a medium mixing bowl, beat eggs and remaining 3/4 cup artificial sweetener. Add lemon juice, remaining 4 tablespoons butter and remaining 1 tablespoon grated lemon peel. Pour mixture into prepared crust. Return to oven for an additional 15 minutes, until lemon filling is set. Let cool completely on a wire rack.

Rhubarb and Apple Crumble

Makes 6 servings

3 C. peeled Granny Smith apples, cut into 3/4" cubes
2 1/2 C. fresh red rhubarb, cut into 3/4" pieces
1/2 C. plus 1/3 C. granulated artificial sweetener
2 T. cornstarch
1/3 C. water or apple juice
1 T. lemon juice

1 tsp. grated lemon peel, optional
3/4 C. quick cooking or rolled oats
1/4 C. raisins
1/4 C. chopped nuts
2 T. butter or margarine, melted
1/2 tsp. cinnamon

Preheat oven to 400°. In a 1 1/2 quart baking dish, combine cubed apples, rhubarb pieces, 1/2 cup artificial sweetener and cornstarch. Mix well until evenly incorporated. In a small bowl, combine water, lemon juice and grated lemon peel. Pour mixture over fruit in baking dish. Cover baking dish with aluminum foil and bake in oven for 20 to 25 minutes or until fruit is tender. Meanwhile, in a medium bowl, combine oats, raisins, chopped nuts, remaining 1/3 cup artificial sweetener, melted butter and cinnamon. Mix until well blended. Remove aluminum foil from baking dish and sprinkle oats mixture over fruit. Return to oven and bake, uncovered, for an additional 8 to 10 minutes or until topping is crisp.

Blueberry Bake

Makes 6 servings

1 C. whole wheat pastry flour
1 tsp. baking powder
1/2 tsp. baking soda
2 T. sugar, divided
1/2 C. low fat buttermilk
2 T. honey

1 T. cornstarch
1 tsp. cinnamon
1 C. water
2 T. lemon juice
3 C. fresh blueberries

Preheat oven to 400°. In a medium bowl, combine whole wheat flour, baking powder, baking soda and 1 tablespoon sugar. Mix until combined and add buttermilk. Mix just until moistened and dough forms a ball. To make filling, in a large saucepan over medium heat, combine remaining 1 tablespoon sugar, honey, cornstarch, cinnamon, water and lemon juice. Mix until smooth and add blueberries. Bring to a simmer for about 10 minutes, stirring gently, until thickened. Spoon mixture into an 8x11" baking dish. Drop buttermilk mixture by tablespoonfuls over blueberries in baking dish. Bake in oven for 20 minutes or until biscuits are lightly browned.

Chocolate Cheesecake

Makes 12 servings

1 (5 1/4 oz.) pkg. sugar-free chocolate graham crackers, crushed	2 1/2 (8 oz.) pkgs. Neufchatel cream cheese, softened
1/3 C. margarine, melted	2 tsp. vanilla
1/4 tsp. cinnamon	3/4 C. plus 2 T. granulated artificial sweetener
1 C. skim milk	1/4 C. cocoa powder
1 (1/4 oz) env. unflavored gelatin	5 (0.6 oz.) sugar-free chocolate wafer bars, coarsely chopped

Preheat oven to 350°. In a medium bowl, combine crushed graham crackers, melted margarine and cinnamon. Mix well and press mixture onto the bottom and 1" up sides of a greased 9" springform pan. Bake in oven for 8 minutes. Remove from oven and let cool on a wire rack. In a small saucepan over low heat, place milk. Sprinkle unflavored gelatin over milk and let sit for 1 minute. Cook for 2 minutes, stirring gently, until gelatin is dissolved. Remove from heat and let cool slightly. In a medium mixing bowl, beat cream cheese until creamy and add vanilla. Add gelatin mixture and beat until smooth. Add artificial sweetener and cocoa powder, beating just until blended. Pour mixture into prepared crust. Cover and chill at least 3 hours or until cheesecake is set. Before serving, garnish with chopped wafers.

Cool Lime Cheesecake

Makes 8 servings

1 C. graham cracker crumbs
3 T. butter or margarine,
   melted
2/3 C. plus 2 T. granulated
   artificial sweetener,
   divided

2 (8 oz.) pkgs. cream cheese,
   softened
3 T. fresh lime juice
1 egg
2 egg whites
1/2 tsp. grated lime peel

Preheat oven to 325°. In a medium bowl, combine graham cracker crumbs, melted butter and 2 tablespoons artificial sweetener. Press mixture onto the bottom and 1/2" up sides of an 8" springform pan or 8" round cake pan. Bake in oven for 8 minutes. In a medium mixing bowl, beat cream cheese and remaining 2/3 cup artificial sweetener until fluffy. Add egg, egg whites, grated lime peel and lime juice and mix until well blended. Pour mixture into prepared crust. Bake in oven for 30 to 35 minutes or until center is almost set. Refrigerate at least 3 hours before serving.

Black Forest Trifle

Makes 12 servings

1 (8 oz.) pkg. sugar-free
  chocolate cake mix
3/4 C. water
1 (1 oz.) box sugar-free
  instant chocolate
  pudding mix
2 C. skim milk

1 (16 oz.) pkg. frozen pitted
  cherries
2 drops red food coloring
2 C. frozen whipped topping,
  thawed
Sugar-free chocolate curls,
  optional

Prepare cake mix according to package directions, using 3/4 cup water. Let cake cool in pan, remove from pan and cut into cubes. Prepare pudding mix according to package directions, using 2 cups skim milk. Chill in refrigerator for at least 30 minutes. Thaw cherries and reserve 1/4 cup cherry juice. In a small bowl, combine cherries, reserved cherry juice and red food coloring. In a 3 quart glass serving bowl, place half of the cake cubes. Spoon half of the cherry mixture over cake cubes and spread 1 cup pudding over cherries. Top with half of the whipped topping. Repeat layers using remaining half of the cake cubes, remaining half of the cherry mixture, remaining 1 cup pudding and remaining half of the whipped topping. If desired, top with chocolate curls. Cover and chill in refrigerator at least 8 hours before serving.

Carrot Cake

Makes 10 servings

7/8 C. flour
1 tsp. baking powder
1/2 tsp. baking soda
1/2 tsp. salt
1/2 tsp. cinnamon
1/4 tsp. ground allspice
2 large egg whites
1/4 C. eggbeaters

**3/8 C. granulated artificial
sweetener**
3 T. margarine, softened
1/2 C. honey
1 tsp. vanilla
3 T. unsweetened applesauce
3 T. vegetable oil
2 1/4 C. finely shredded carrots
1/3 C. chopped walnuts

Preheat oven to 350°. In a medium bowl, combine flour, baking powder, baking soda, salt, cinnamon and ground allspice and set aside. In a small bowl, whisk together egg whites and egg beaters and set aside. In a large bowl, combine artificial sweetener, margarine, honey, vanilla, applesauce and vegetable oil. Add egg mixture and stir until well combined. Stir in flour mixture, shredded carrots and chopped walnuts. Pour mixture into a greased 8 cup loaf pan and bake for 40 to 45 minutes or until a toothpick inserted in center of cake comes out clean.

Sugar-Free Apple Pie

Makes 8 servings

3 T. cornstarch	6 C. sliced green apples
1 T. cinnamon	2 (9") pie pastry crusts
1 (12 oz.) can unsweetened frozen apple juice concentrate, thawed	

Preheat oven to 350°. In a small bowl, whisk together cornstarch, cinnamon and 1/3 cup apple juice concentrate and set aside. In a large saucepan over medium heat, combine remaining apple juice concentrate and sliced apples. Simmer for about 10 minutes, until apples are tender. Stir in cornstarch mixture and continue to simmer until thickened. Remove from heat. Place one pie pastry crust in a 9" pie plate. Spoon apple mixture into pie crust and cover with remaining pastry crust. Pinch the edges of the crust together to seal the filling and flute the edges. Cut steam vents in top crust. Bake in oven for 45 minutes or until crust is golden brown.

Apple Cranberry Streussel Pie

Makes 8 servings

1 (9") pie pastry crust
1 3/4 C. granulated artificial sweetener, divided
1 T. cornstarch
1 1/2 C. fresh or frozen cranberries, thawed
1 C. apple cider or unsweetened apple juice
1 3/4 tsp. cinnamon, divided

3/4 tsp. nutmeg, divided
1/4 tsp. salt
5 C. peeled, cored and sliced apples
1/4 C. quick cooking or rolled oats
3 T. flour
4 T. cold butter or margarine, cut into pieces

Preheat oven to 400°. Roll pie pastry crust into a 10" circle. Place pastry in pan and trim and flute the edge. In a small saucepan over medium heat, combine 1 cup artificial sweetener and cornstarch. Stir in cranberries and apple cider. Bring to a boil, reduce heat and let simmer for about 1 minute, stirring constantly, until thickened. In a small bowl, combine 1/4 cup artificial sweetener, 3/4 teaspoon cinnamon, 1/4 teaspoon nutmeg and salt. Place sliced apples in a large bowl and sprinkle cinnamon mixture over apples and toss until evenly coated. Pour cranberry mixture over apples and mix gently. Arrange fruit in pie pastry. To make topping, in a small bowl, combine oats, flour, remaining 1/2 cup artificial sweetener, remaining 1 teaspoon cinnamon and remaining 1/2 teaspoon nutmeg. Using a pastry blender, cut in butter pieces. Sprinkle topping over fruit in pie crust. Bake in oven for 50 to 60 minutes or until apples are tender and crust is golden. Cover pie loosely with aluminum foil during last 20 to 30 minutes of baking time to prevent excess browning.

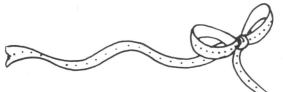

Fresh Strawberry Cream Pie

Makes 8 servings

1 qt. fresh strawberries
7 T. granulated artificial sweetener, divided
1 1/2 (8 oz.) pkgs. cream cheese, softened

1/2 C. vanilla nonfat yogurt
1 1/2 T. lemon juice
1 (9") pie pastry crust

Set aside 1 large strawberry. Remove stems from all remaining strawberries. Slice enough of the strawberries to make 1 cup. In a small bowl, toss sliced strawberries with 1 tablespoon artificial sweetener and set aside. In a medium mixing bowl, beat cream cheese, yogurt, lemon juice and remaining 6 tablespoons artificial sweetener. Place pie pastry crust in a 9" pie pan and spread half of the cream cheese mixture over bottom of pie crust. Top with sliced strawberries and cover with remaining half of the cream cheese mixture. Cut remaining stemless strawberries in half. Place halved strawberries, cut side down, over cream cheese mixture around outer edge of pie with strawberries pointing toward the center. Make several slits in the reserved large strawberry and press gently to form a fan. Place fanned strawberry in center of pie.

Pumpkin Pie

Makes 8 servings

1 (9") pie pastry crust
1 (15 oz.) can pumpkin puree
1 (12 oz.) can fat free
    evaporated milk
3 eggs
3/4 C. granulated artificial
    sweetener

1 tsp. vanilla
1 tsp. cinnamon
1/4 tsp. ground ginger
1/4 tsp. nutmeg
1/4 tsp. salt

Preheat oven to 400°. Roll pie pastry crust into a 10" circle. Place pastry in pan and trim and flute the edge. In a medium mixing bowl, beat together pumpkin puree, evaporated milk and eggs. Beat well and add artificial sweetener, vanilla, cinnamon, ground ginger, nutmeg and salt. Pour mixture into prepared pastry shell. Bake in oven for 35 to 40 minutes or until a knife inserted in center of pie comes out clean. Remove from oven and let cool on a wire rack.

Index

Cookies

Cakes

Pies & Pastries

No-Bake

Fancy Schmancy

Diabetic